STARGATE
ATLANTIS™

THE OFFICIAL COMPANION
SEASON 1

STARGATE: ATLANTIS: THE OFFICIAL COMPANION SEASON 1
1 84576 116 2

Published by
Titan Books
A division of
Titan Publishing Group Ltd
144 Southwark St
London
SE1 0UP

First edition July 2005
1 3 5 7 9 10 8 6 4 2

DEDICATION
For Mum, Dad and Jonathan — I wouldn't change you guys for the world.

ACKNOWLEDGEMENTS
Thanks to everyone on the *Stargate: Atlantis* sets and in the production offices who helped me put this together, including everyone who spent time being interviewed and sourcing pictures when you are all so busy. Thanks to Brad Wright and Robert C. Cooper for always being gracious with your time under such great pressures, and to Joe Flanigan for penning the Foreword. Thanks to the wonderful Brigitte Prochaska for putting up with my numerous interview requests, and also to Carole Appleby for helping out in the latter stages. Thanks to Karol Mora at MGM, for being hugely cool without knowing it. Finally, thanks to Jo Boylett at Titan for hammering this into shape where needed. You all rock!

Titan Books would also like to thank all the *Stargate: Atlantis* cast and crew. We're also grateful to Elaine Piechowski and Karol Mora at MGM for their continuing help.

Did you enjoy this book? We love to hear from our readers. Please e-mail us at: readerfeedback@titanemail.com or write to Reader Feedback at the above address. To subscribe to our regular newsletter for up-to-the-minute news, great offers and competitions, email: titan-news@titanemail.com

Visit our website: **www.titanbooks.com**

Printed and bound in Great Britain by MPG, Bodmin, Cornwall.

STARGATE ATLANTIS

THE OFFICIAL COMPANION

SEASON 1   SHARON GOSLING

STARGATE: ATLANTIS DEVELOPED FOR TELEVISION BY
BRAD WRIGHT AND ROBERT C. COOPER

TITAN BOOKS

CONTENTS

FOREWORD

A few months ago, while I was picking up my five-year-old boy from school, I was approached by one of his teachers. She asked if we could speak privately. We walked under the large cedar tree in the schoolyard. "Your son, Aidan, has told the other boys that his father flies through space and kills bad guys." She spoke with crossed arms and a crisp British accent. Apparently, the boys were having a my-daddy-is-bigger-than-your-daddy conversation when Aidan dropped the bomb. His schoolmates were understandably impressed and apparently not the least bit confused. Nonetheless, the teacher's message was clear: bring your boy back to the Earth... please.

As I loaded Aidan into the car, I grappled how best to broach the subject. I rolled down the windows, turned on a little Led Zeppelin... and drove home. Who am I to crush a small boy's big imagination?

On its face, this story appears to be about a child who possesses a rather blurry distinction between fiction and reality (laced with the all too perishable phenomenon of father worship). Nonetheless, it reveals a more basic desire we all have: to imagine a world other than the one we live in. It is precisely that impulse that makes sci-fi, and the *Stargate* shows — *Atlantis* and *SG-1* — in particular, so popular. Some believe sci-fi is simply metaphor. Others say it is a glimpse at the inevitable future. In an increasingly divided world, perhaps it is the fantasy of humankind uniting under a common cause to deal with the dark unknown we all face. More importantly, for me, it's a *lot of work*.

The day begins around 5 to 6am. I shave, take a shower, and hope the kids are up so I can see them before I disappear. My trusted confidant and driver, Dave Byerly, has the car running with coffee and a newspaper. We have our ritual conversation about sleep, or lack thereof. We make some offensive jokes and fantasize about winning the lottery. By then we've arrived at the Bridge Studios, which is bustling with typical movie-making activity. Camera trucks are being jostled into position, off-duty aliens are getting their breakfast, and ADs are already panicking about the day's schedule. I am then whisked off to a blocking, followed by make-up, a quick change and BAM... we're shooting.

If I get the opportunity, I try to make my way to the production office once a day. The food is better and there are no loitering aliens. This would also be the natural habitat of the elusive and mysterious breed of scriveners who have been providing *Stargate SG-1* fans with an endless stream of good stories (208 episodes and counting). Some of them possess suspiciously large collections of animated figurines. Martin Gero's office is populated by Muppets. And yes, Martin, they are real. Joe Malozzi seeks refuge with his friends, the Simpsons. (Brad Wright has replaced his figurines with Awards.) One wonders how they develop so many original storylines.

And yet, with all of its resident weirdness, it is one of the greatest places I've ever worked. It is perhaps a cliché for us in the entertainment business to thank people, but

for this, there is a very good reason. Producing a television show is a monumental creative and logistical accomplishment. I, therefore, say thank you first and foremost to Brad Wright and Robert Cooper for being brilliant and unusually receptive executive producers, damn good writers, and maintaining a sense of play in the *very* serious world of today's television industry. Hank Cohen for offering me the job. We miss you. John Smith for his Swiss-like precision managing production. All of the writers for their humor and originality, and not turning us into Muppets… yet. Torri Higginson for her professionalism and patience. David Hewlett for possessing a sicker sense of humor than myself and being an OK actor. Rachel Luttrell for putting up with our sense of humor and being, well, very beautiful. Paul McGillion for torturing himself with a Scottish accent. All of the crew for their hard work and affability. David Byerly for driving me to and from work everyday and getting me to believe, at no small price, I can win the lottery. And last, but never least, I want to thank my wife Katherine and our kids, Aidan and Truman, for filling the cloud-covered Northwest with so much sun. Å

JOE FLANIGAN
Vancouver, June 2005

A NEW GATE OPENS...

WATER GATE

"All right, here we go. We are about to try and make a connection. We have been able to predict how much power this will take, and we may only get one chance at this."
— Weir

Can lightning ever strike twice? That question must have been asked numerous times in studio and network boardrooms as *Stargate: Atlantis*, the most high-profile science fiction television spin-off event since *Star Trek: The Next Generation*, came slowly into existence. For several record-breaking years, Brad Wright and Robert C. Cooper's *Stargate SG-1* had been top of the tree at the US Sci Fi Channel. The series had been co-created by Wright and his producing partner Jonathan Glassner following the success of Roland Emmerich and Dean Devlin's blockbuster movie *Stargate*, and had already built a considerable following on Showtime. At the conclusion of its fifth year, however, *Stargate SG-1*, already a veteran series, moved to the Sci Fi Channel and immediately surpassed itself. Catapulted into a wider sphere, shown at regular times and advertised appropriately, it quickly became the network's highest-rated show. Thus the season that had originally been mooted as the series' swansong actually assured its renewed longevity — for just as long as the cast were happy to remain in the roles that they had already filled for more than half a decade.

Actors are after all, by trade, a nomadic bunch — roles come and go, particularly in the fickle world of television. No actor expects to be playing the same role for more than a few years, and for the most part no actor wants to. Job security aside, actors enjoy frequent change and being able to explore different characters just the same as any other creative spirit. When it seemed clear that *Stargate SG-1* had the capacity to run and run, two other things also became apparent to the executive producers — one, that not all their stars would be content to stay in the same place for the best part of ten years, and two, that the show would, beyond its seventh year, become shockingly expensive to produce. The *Stargate SG-1* cast had, since the early days of the show, become massive stars, not only in the US but also overseas, and thus the annual wage bill for the company naturally continued to increase to match their market worth. However, though the annual budget the producers were given to make the show was also increasing, it was in no way enough to cover the shortfall, and the producers knew that eventually this would show through on screen.

From fans to network executives, no one wanted the *Stargate SG-1* universe to end. But neither could the original show continue in the same vein forever. So how best to follow the phenomenal success of *Stargate SG-1*? How, even, could the producers round off the show to the satisfaction of the viewers, not to mention themselves? Thus began the search for the perfect way of continuing on from SG-1's adventures — a search that was neither straightforward nor quick.

"Let's see," says executive producer Robert C. Cooper, considering the days before *Stargate: Atlantis* sparked into existence. "Back in season five, when we thought *Stargate SG-1* was going to end, Brad [Wright] concocted a plan — the first of many, as it would turn out. We would finish *Stargate SG-1* and make a feature film. It was actually slightly more complicated than that," he explains briefly, "involving the business end of things and words like 'infrastructure'. But the bottom line is, a movie seemed like a slam dunk for a franchise that had become an international success and started as a feature in the first place."

Of course, as everyone now knows, season five was nowhere near the end of the wormhole for *Stargate SG-1*. Though it had reached as far as it would go on Showtime, there was another channel waiting in the wings, looking for a hit show to spearhead its slate of original programming.

Above: Michael Shanks as Daniel Jackson in *Stargate SG-1*'s 'Lost City' part one.

"The Sci Fi Channel jumped in and picked up season six," Cooper continues. "Feature on hold. So, we decided to make the film at the end of season six — what would *surely* be the last season of the series. Then we aired on Sci Fi, and the ratings kicked ass," he laughs, "so talk of season seven pushed the feature back again. The story was to revolve around the search for the lost city of the Ancients, and was to end on Earth. SG-1 was going to find the lost city on Earth and save the day from Anubis. But by now, the end of season six was breaking all of the Sci Fi Channel's ratings records, and talk not only of season eight but also a spin-off series was starting to float around."

With all this going on, the producers were left with a serious dilemma, as the whole of season seven had been planned to lead up to this momentous discovery of the

Ancients' 'lost city'. "The 'Lost City' script was supposed to be a bridge between *Stargate SG-1* and either a series of movies or another television show that was not supposed to run concurrently with *Stargate SG-1*," Cooper explains. "The story could not be pushed back any more — we were going to spend a whole year building up to it, and we just couldn't stall any more. After much consternation, Brad and I rewrote the 'Lost City' feature script into the season seven finale, and changed the concept. SG-1 would find an outpost built by the Ancients who left Earth millions of years before in their giant flying city. That city went to another galaxy and encountered an entirely new villain."

The original story of this 'lost city' had now been in the heads of the two executive producers since mid-season five. As a result, revising the story to not only keep *Stargate SG-1* going far beyond its originally imagined life-span, but also introduce an entirely new show in the same universe, involved completely revolutionizing the basis of the script.

"It changed a great deal, actually," Brad Wright reveals. "I had planned for Atlantis to be under the ice of Antarctica, supplanting the SGC. When we realized that Stargate Command was going to continue, Rob suggested that the city could have actually left Earth for the Pegasus Galaxy. I think the series is much better for that change."

Below: Richard Dean Anderson as Jack O'Neill in *Stargate SG-1*'s 'Lost City' part two.

In fact, removing Atlantis from Earth and placing it in an environment difficult to reach from the SGC formed the key aspect of the *Stargate: Atlantis* spin-off. "We wanted the new show, which was going to have to co-exist with *Stargate SG-1*, to have a distinct life of its own," Cooper explains. "We decided to set it in another galaxy so that the audience wouldn't be constantly wondering why SG-1 wasn't being called in to save the day when our new Atlantis heroes got into trouble. Also, we felt that we had told a lot of stories about the Goa'uld, and we wanted to wipe the slate clean."

Though the concept of *Stargate SG-1* spinning off either into a series of movies or into a new show had now been gathering pace for several years, getting the go-ahead to put *Stargate: Atlantis* into production actually came very suddenly. Seeing an opportunity to launch another hit from the *Stargate SG-1* stable while the veteran parent show was still on air, the Sci Fi Channel decided that they wanted the spin-off to launch in summer 2004, alongside *Stargate SG-1*'s eighth season. This decision came incredibly late — so late, in fact, that *Stargate SG-1*'s seventh season had wrapped filming and all but the writers and producers had left Vancouver's Bridge Studios for the winter. Putting two series into production for summer débuts would be demand-

Above: Major John Sheppard follows in Jack O'Neill's footsteps.

Above: The Atlantis expedition prepare to leave from Earth's Stargate Command in *Stargate: Atlantis'* pilot episode.

ing enough — that one of them would be launching from scratch, and as of November there was no pilot script let alone a cast, standing sets or a long-term plan, was something else entirely.

"We got the green light to start writing on November 17th," Brad Wright recalls. "We began shooting at the end of February. I know there's a perception that I went away for a year and wrote the pilot — not true. I had ideas, certainly, but I didn't set pen to paper, metaphorically speaking, until the series was ordered and I had a deal to do it. That's when Rob and I began the real work."

Martin Wood had been directing on *Stargate SG-1* since the show's first season, and was drafted in by the two executive producers to direct the *Stargate: Atlantis* pilot. He still fondly recalls the various stages of evolution that led to the series' birth.

"Brad, Robert and I had been working on the *Stargate SG-1* movie," he explains. "We had been talking about it for a long time, and they had asked me to direct 'Lost City', which was to be the movie — this was before anyone had started talking about a spin-off. Unfortunately," Wood laughs, "the movie was really, really good, but no one will ever see it now! I read a couple of drafts of the script thinking, 'This is going to be amazing!' Then, of course, we got season seven and then season eight, and

Stargate SG-1 just kept going on. So they turned the feature script into the 'Lost City' story, but kept parts of it for the *Stargate: Atlantis* pilot. They asked me if I would be interested in doing the pilot and I jumped at that, of course. And in a very short period of time, approximately from November to January, *Stargate: Atlantis* was born."

Being involved from such an early stage allowed Wood to be attendant as Wright and Cooper beat out the specifics of the *Stargate: Atlantis* series and its opening double-length episode, 'Rising'. This process, the director says, was an eye-opening demonstration of how an episode of television comes together when it has input from two of the most well respected executives in the industry.

"I was sitting in on meetings and talking about what was going to happen," explains Wood, "but if you ever sat in on a story meeting with Robert and Brad, you would see an amazing thing happen. I've watched it happen so many times, and it is still incredible to me. They sit there. Ideas are being thrown around and suddenly Brad or Robert will stand up and say, 'Okay, this is what it's going to be.' And they start to spin out three acts of a story. The other writers are sitting there with their mouths open! It happened with Carl Binder, and with Martin Gero. They sit there, and you look at them while they're watching this, and [you can see] they're thinking, 'I could never do this!'" Wood says with a laugh, "because it really is stunning to watch. As they're talking, these stories come out of the spin. And this is what happened with 'Rising'. They would go back and forth, Robert would say something and then Brad would say something, and then Robert would say something else and then Brad would say something else, and they're correcting each other and then the other one goes, 'Oh right, okay then, let's do this...' And so, 'Rising' was born in two or three of these meetings. That's something no other human can really do — it has to be these two guys. So I was involved to the extent that you *can* be involved with Brad and Robert," he says, laughing again, "where for the most part they have the story in their heads. What you're doing as a director is tweaking the vision that they have, and adding your own two cents' worth to each scene."

"Rob and I both have strong personalities," says Wright, "and are unused to working with a writing partner. But we've worked together for coming up on nine years now. That goes a long way! Sure, we debated things, and rewrote each other back and forth, but whenever either one of us felt strongly about something enough to fight for it, that's the way we went."

Even once the pilot had been drafted, *Stargate: Atlantis* still continued to evolve quite considerably. Martin Wood, for one, was still hoping to keep much of the 'Lost City' movie that he had originally envisioned filming.

"It was a really interesting collaborative process once the first draft came out," Wood remembers. "I was still holding on to parts of 'Lost City', the feature script, and saying, 'Oh, what if we did this? It would be so neat to do this...'" the director grins. "At the very beginning, I said, 'Well, we have to use the girl from [season six episode]

'Frozen' in the very first scenes, as she was the Ancient that was left behind,' and so suddenly that gets written into the script."

This evolution didn't just apply to the pilot itself, but to the series proper, which even once the pilot had been written was in a state of flux. "The key elements that I think made the show real in our minds was the idea that it was set in another galaxy, the Wraith, and the city as an island," Cooper explains. "Of course, these were just concepts that continued to evolve right through production. We discussed potential arenas and elements of stories that would naturally flow out of the concept for the series, but a large part of actually writing episodes is the characters. Until the pilot was written no one, including Brad and I, had any real idea of who the characters were and what they would sound like. After the pilot was written we started developing episode ideas, but it wasn't until we had cast the show and started to hear the voices come out of the actors' mouths that any really productive writing could take place."

Casting for a new television show is a tricky business, as inappropriate casting

Below: Sheppard confronts the mysteries of the Pegasus Galaxy

can ruin a show from the start. *Stargate: Atlantis* was a different proposition to *Stargate SG-1*, which had only ever had four main characters and three or four recurring supporting roles at most. The spin-off was set to be quite different, with a regular cast of five and many other characters who would recur repeatedly throughout season one.

Finding the right faces and voices for *Stargate: Atlantis* proved a considerable challenge, as Cooper explains: "The only other decision besides story and concept that makes a huge difference is casting. Obviously, there were going to be new heroes and new faces on screen. That was going to make *Stargate: Atlantis* different [from *Stargate SG-1*] in huge ways and ultimately would make or break the series."

"What is most daunting about casting a TV series is that if you get it wrong, you may not have a show," Brad Wright agrees. "The best writing, directing and visual effects in the world won't help you if you don't put together a cast people want to invite into their homes every week. Fortunately, I think we managed to do that."

Below: Guest star Robert Patrick with Joe Flanigan and Rainbow Sun Francks during the filming of 'Rising'.

WATER GATE

Above: A computer-generated view of Atlantis.

They certainly did, but it wasn't an easy process. For a start, the executives ruled out casting any 'star names', as is often done with fledgling series, on the basis that they were already experiencing the financial pressures associated with star names in *Stargate SG-1*, and with the reduced budget that necessarily goes with a show's first year, to do so would be tantamount to shooting themselves in the foot.

"We couldn't afford any big-name actors," Cooper jokes good-naturedly. "Maybe that's not so funny, but actually, there was a lot of talk about so-called 'name' actors. Brad and I felt that the *Stargate SG-1* franchise was the 'name' that would get people to tune in. We're glad that the network and studio ultimately agreed, because as much as we want our show to be a success, and names certainly get you in the door, we feel that good actors create great long-lasting characters. We wanted to cast the best actors we could find for the roles, and we think we did. The fact that *Stargate: Atlantis* continued to beat *Stargate SG-1* in the ratings [during the first year] seems to suggest that we may have been right. And now, in the world of science fiction anyway, the cast of *Stargate: Atlantis* *are* big name actors."

There were several aspects that made casting *Stargate: Atlantis* more difficult than it might otherwise have been, the first of these being that because of the late go-ahead and the launch date, the producers were looking for their cast at the same time as every other new show in North America. The early part of each new year is known in the television industry as 'pilot season', as each network commissions a plethora of new shows at the same time and then chooses the best to be picked up for the programming year. At this time of year, every actor and actress not currently in a permanent role spends most of their time auditioning for numerous series, which means that if there is more than one set of producers interested in signing the same actor, some will doubtless be disappointed and discover that their choice has signed just an hour or two earlier for another show.

"It was difficult," Cooper says, "especially since the networks have concocted a brilliant system whereby every actor in the world auditions for every potential television show at the same time! Now we aren't technically a network show, so the fact that we happened to be casting *Stargate: Atlantis* during pilot season was coincidental and unfortunate timing. Not that we didn't see endless streams of auditions which had

Below: The cast of *Stargate: Atlantis*, season one.

WATER GATE

already been pared down from even more by our fearless US casting director Paul Weber," the executive producer adds with a dry laugh, "who, by the way, never gets enough credit, as well as our Canadian casting directors Sean Cossey and Stuart Aiken. You see, the other issue is that Brad and I are Canadian, and we shoot our show in Canada. Not only do we like to hire Canadians wherever possible, but we also benefit from that through tax credits that make the show possible."

As the casting process continued and the two executive producers got ever closer to completing their ensemble, one face resolutely failed to present itself. This was the character of 'Doctor Ingram', a somewhat excitable scientist who was to join the Atlantis expedition as an expert on celestial mechanics and the Stargate, amongst other things. As the opening day of shooting drew ever nearer, and repeated auditions failed to find an actor that both the writers and the network executives could agree on, the production began to think that perhaps it wasn't that they were not finding the right actor, but that in fact they had brought in the wrong character.

"I kept thinking, this should be McKay," recalls Martin Wood. "I walked into Brad's office and said, 'This really should be McKay.' He said, 'Well, MGM is looking for someone different, but I feel it should be McKay too,' and Robert was saying the same thing. We all kept saying, 'This feels much more like it should be McKay!' Finally, we pushed the button on McKay."

Thus, a character that had appeared as a brief guest role for three episodes of *Stargate SG-1* suddenly became a regular on *Stargate: Atlantis*. To everyone's relief, actor David Hewlett was able to take the part, and a day after filming had started on 'Rising', he signed his deal and arrived on set. Though that opening script was not rewritten for the character of McKay, Cooper reports that his addition, alongside the presence of *Stargate SG-1* regulars Richard Dean Anderson (Jack O'Neill) and Michael Shanks (Daniel Jackson) really helped kick the spin-off into action.

"It's always harder imagining something from nothing," he says. "When you see the actors and hear their voices, it's much easier to write dialogue for them. But we still had O'Neill and Daniel crossing over in the pilot, and we had created McKay during season four of *Stargate SG-1*. Weir was a character we developed in 'Lost City'. So it wasn't all brand new. Still, you start with big picture ideas and whittle down to specifics. Who are these people? What are their stories? What do they care about and how do they express themselves?"

"In series television, you have to think of the whole, not just the individual parts," adds Brad Wright. "You're trying to create a dynamic that will service storytelling. For example, Joe [Flanigan]'s dry wit and easy-going manner plays well opposite McKay's more frenetic energy."

Thanks to the cast they had assembled, and with the dailies from the filming of 'Rising', the characters soon solidified in the heads of the writers, and allowed them to continue to build on what was to come.

"You do go in with certain intentions," explains Robert Cooper. "For example, we originally hoped that the Weir/Sheppard relationship would be the Jackson/O'Neill relationship but in reverse, with the civilian being in charge of the military man. But as you have probably seen, that relationship has evolved very differently. In fact, Sheppard and Weir don't clash much at all, and the conflict we envisioned between them doesn't seem to work when we try. Part of this is because Weir is not on the team, and part of it is because of the tone of *Atlantis*. People seem to want to see our heroes fighting the Wraith, not each other. For some reason it just seems more petty on *Stargate: Atlantis* — maybe because it's an expedition and they are so far from home. They only have each other, and must stick together. Plus, the more amusingly abrasive dynamic between McKay and just about everyone else evolved and gave us the edge that the Daniel/Jack relationship was giving us in *Stargate SG-1*. We start with certain ideas, and at some point the actors, the characters and the series take on a life of their own." Å

Below: Dr Elizabeth Weir boldly goes where no diplomat has gone before…

THE EPISODES

"You are the world's best and brightest. And in the light of the adventure we are about to embark on, you are also the bravest. I hope we all return one day, having discovered a whole new realm for humanity to explore. But as all of you know, we may never be able to return home." — *Weir*

SEASON 1 REGULAR CAST:

Joe Flanigan (Major John Sheppard)

Torri Higginson (Dr Elizabeth Weir)

Rachel Luttrell (Teyla Emmagan)

Rainbow Sun Francks (Lieutenant Aiden Ford)

David Hewlett (Dr Rodney McKay)

RISING (I)

WRITTEN BY: Brad Wright and Robert C. Cooper

DIRECTED BY: Martin Wood

GUEST CAST: Richard Dean Anderson (General Jack O'Neill), Michael Shanks (Dr Daniel Jackson), Robert Patrick (Colonel Marshall Sumner), Paul McGillion (Dr Beckett), Craig Veroni (Dr Grodin), Garwin Sanford (Simon), Christopher Heyerdahl (Halling)

While investigating the Ancient outpost in Antarctica, Daniel Jackson makes an exciting discovery. He knows where the 'lost' city of Atlantis is — and he knows how to get there. Assembling an international team of scientists and flanked by US marines led by Colonel Sumner, Dr Elizabeth Weir prepares to launch an expedition to the distant Pegasus Galaxy. They are joined by Major John Sheppard, a disgraced pilot who has the Ancient gene required to activate the advanced Ancient technology. It is possible that this could be a one-way trip — the amount of power required to activate a wormhole to another galaxy is immense — but all appreciate the import of such a mission. Stepping through the Stargate, the team finds themselves directly inside Atlantis. The city, as if alert to their arrival, begins to power up — they find science laboratories, living quarters, and even three space ships, all of which has been submerged beneath an ocean for centuries, hiding from a terrible enemy. Then, McKay discovers a severe problem. If they don't do something quickly, the shield will collapse and they will all drown. Since they don't have enough power to open a wormhole back to Earth, Weir orders Sumner and his team, along with Sheppard, to find a local planet to which they can evacuate. Traveling to a planet called Athosia, they meet a peaceful race led by a young woman, Teyla Emmagan. When Sumner asks permission to stay in the ruins of a nearby city, Teyla tells them of a fearful race called the Wraith, whom her people believe will return if they enter the city. As if to prove a point, before the team can return to Atlantis, three ships arrive through the Stargate. The Wraith have returned.

SHEPPARD: I think people who don't want to fly are crazy.
O'NEILL: And I think people who don't want to go through the Stargate are equally as whacked.

The start of filming on the *Stargate: Atlantis* pilot put in motion the wheels of a great machine, at the helm of which was veteran television director and *Stargate SG-1* crew regular Martin Wood. Having been present as the spin-off evolved from the earliest ideas of executive producers Brad Wright and Robert C. Cooper, it was now Wood's task to turn their vision into screen reality.

"We shot for twenty-five days," Wood says of the two-part pilot. "The nice thing about being able to shoot for that amount of time is that you can take time establishing things and dealing with character development. You can't do that in a seven-day

Opposite: Weir discovers a surprise gift from Jack O'Neill.

Above: The fledgling team find their leader.

shoot," he adds, speaking of the usual amount of time scheduled for an episode of an established series. "With this pilot, we were able to play around a little with the look of things — we were able to light [the sets] for a little longer, and rehearse a little longer. It was the extended period of time that gave us the chance to tweak things that we wouldn't normally in the course of regular shooting."

Wood also had the benefit of a bigger budget, allowing him to film some grand sequences, like O'Neill and Sheppard's opening helicopter flight from McMurdo to the Ancient outpost. "I loved that," says Wood. "It was the Pemberton Glacier. One of the reasons we used that area is that there are actually a couple of places you can look pretty much 360 degrees and all you see is snow. We thought it would be the perfect place to simulate Antarctica. We went up there on a scout to figure out what we were going to do, and then we loaded Richard Dean Anderson and Joe Flanigan and the crew into four different helicopters and flew up. We shot for an entire day, and just as it was getting dark we all piled back in and flew home. Everyone had the *best* time."

The director feels that this sentiment typified the shoot, despite the understandable nerves of the new cast as they settled into their roles: "Everybody was certainly incredibly nervous, because they didn't have a handle on the characters. The only person who had an established character was David Hewlett, and he came in very late in the day — actually, the day after we started shooting."

To aid everyone in this regard, Wood spent a lot of time with the actors before the cameras started rolling, helping them hone their initial ideas of their characters. Interestingly, this preparation was helped by a request from the network. "As we started shooting, the network [Sci-Fi Channel] said, 'We really need something that identifies our four major characters'," Wood reveals. "That was the little montage that you see at the beginning, before the expedition leaves. That was not in the original script, and Brad didn't really want it in there, because he said, 'It gives away who the characters are before we need to know, before a team has been made.' But interestingly, it gave the characters a little bit of back-story that they wouldn't normally have had."

WEIR: Seriously, doctor, calm down — you're embarrassing me.
McKAY: I've never been so excited in my entire life.

In editing the first part of 'Rising' to its final form, Wood reports that several longer scenes had to be cut down in order for the episode to come in at the right length, including an entire thread that tied into the team's first encounter with the Athosians.

"Ford and Sheppard are standing outside the tent, and Ford has just given a Swiss Army Knife to two of the Athosians that are standing there," he recalls. "There was this whole explanation of what you can do with a Swiss Army Knife, and there was this big crane shot that moved across the lake and you saw them sitting there explaining it; it was very funny. You see a remnant of that when Colonel Sumner walks outside and tells Ford to head back to the Stargate. There are two guys standing there, and if you're wondering what they have in their hands, they're holding the pocket knife. At the very end of the scene, as Sumner walks away, Ford walks over and says, 'Give me back my knife,' and takes it and walks away. There was also a thread about the power bar. There was this whole thing about, 'And what is this?' and Sheppard says, 'It's a power bar, it gives you energy.' Teyla throws it back to Sheppard [later] as they are running through the woods. He says something like, 'Oh, this is tiring,' and she says, 'Maybe you need one of your power bars.' It was a character piece for Sheppard and a little bit for Ford."

For Brad Wright, the knowledge that the spin-off was up and running was less reassuring than it could have been, simply because of what *Stargate SG-1* and *Stargate: Atlantis* filming simultaneously meant for his schedule. "My first thoughts upon seeing dailies for the first time, if I'm completely honest," says Wright candidly, "was the panic that set in knowing I had to make eighteen more hours of this show after 'Rising' was finished shooting. As for the look of the dailies themselves, I was delighted." Å

Classified Information

The Pemberton Glacier previously doubled for Antarctica in the season one *Stargate SG-1* episode 'Solitudes', which was also directed by Martin Wood.

RISING (II)

WRITTEN BY: Brad Wright / Robert C. Cooper

DIRECTED BY: Martin Wood

GUEST CAST: Robert Patrick (Colonel Marshall Sumner), Paul McGillion (Dr Carson Beckett), Craig Veroni (Dr Peter Grodin), Christopher Heyerdahl (Halling), Andee Frizzell (Female Wraith)

The Wraith attack. Sumner's team are unable to stop them, confused by apparitions that appear on the ground. Teyla tells Sheppard that the Wraith are able to make their victims see things that aren't there, so Sumner directs all their firepower at the attacking ships. The marines succeed in downing one craft, but it's not enough — both Sumner and Teyla are taken by the Wraith, who then leave through the gate, though not before Lieutenant Ford memorizes the symbols on the DHD. Sheppard returns to Atlantis with the survivors to find Weir about to order an evacuation — McKay hasn't been able to solve the power problem and the shield is about to fail. As the shield collapses, however, an automatic safety mechanism raises the entire city clear of the waves. Sheppard persuades a reluctant Weir to allow him to mount a rescue mission. Using one of the Ancient space ships, Sheppard and his team infiltrate a massive Wraith ship, freeing Teyla and her people. Sumner, however, is being interrogated by a female Wraith — a creature that feeds by sucking a person's life-force out with their hands. Most of the Wraith are hibernating, waiting for their human food source to grow in numbers — but the news of another galaxy where life flourishes unchecked has excited the monster. Sheppard shoots Sumner dead in the belief that this is what the Colonel wanted. He also executes the Wraith female, who informs him that with her death, the others will reawaken. Sheppard and his team escape to the relative safety of Atlantis, but they have made a great enemy.

Ford: I thought that was the hard part.
Sheppard: Crap. I don't think we've gotten to the hard part yet.

Whereas the first part of 'Rising' spent time getting the Atlantis expedition to the Pegasus Galaxy and introducing the regular *Stargate: Atlantis* cast, the second part of the pilot was an all-out action ride that introduced Sheppard and his team to the most horrifying aspect of the Pegasus Galaxy — the Wraith.

For Brad Wright, delaying the appearance of the Wraith until late in the second half of the pilot was an important part of setting them up as the show's main nemesis. "We wanted to build up the mystery of the Wraith," he explains. To this end, the audience's first introduction to the Wraith is not face-to-face but through a sighting of the predator's terrifying ships and aptitude for mind-manipulation.

Opposite: The Wraith introduce themselves to Sheppard.

MISSION ⊙ DEBRIEF

=== SGC ===

The Ancients

The original sentient species to evolve on Earth, the Ancients were hugely advanced technologically. Having created the Stargates and populated Earth and beyond, they extended their explorations to the Pegasus Galaxy. Building the city of Atlantis, they began to research other planes of existence. However, at some point they encountered (or perhaps even inadvertently created) the Wraith, a terrible enemy that overran Pegasus and besieged Atlantis. Realizing the battle was lost, the Ancients submerged the city and returned to Earth, hoping to one day return to Pegasus. Back on Earth, they learned how to leave their corporeal bodies and Ascend into beings of pure energy, leaving Earth free to experience its second evolution of sentient life — human beings in their current state, distant descendents of the Ancients.

Martin Wood reveals that the Wraith's ghostly attempts to trick Sumner's marines was actually filmed to be much longer than ended up being seen on screen. "We're on the Wraith planet and we're trying to escape," the director explains, "we have Athosians with us, and we get away. Ford is told to go back to guard our six, and what happens is that Teyla senses that the Wraith are near. She turns around and goes back, and there was a scene with Rainbow sitting in the forest and he's got all these phantoms roving around him. He's not familiar enough with them to know what they're not real, so he's spinning around shooting at things that aren't there. There was this huge steadycam shot that moved right around him. It was a very neat scene, but it really didn't give us anything that we didn't get from Teyla just coming up to him."

SHEPPARD: I'm beginning to think you're right. I have made things much worse. I haven't made us many more friends out there.

WEIR: No? Look around you.

Later, of course, the audience get a very real introduction to the horrors of this new enemy.

For Robert Cooper, the enormity of producing the *Stargate: Atlantis* pilot did necessitate changes even as filming of the episode progressed. "The concept of the

Wraith and the look of the city was constantly evolving and required a lot of attention," Cooper explains, detailing the weight of components that made up the pilot. "There were more VFX shots in the two hour pilot than we had ever attempted before in that much screen time. There were numerous huge sets, costumes, new props, make-up. Obviously, in the short time we had, there had to be some compromises."

Cooper still reports that he was very happy with the finished result — especially once the finishing touches had been added to the final cut. "The cast was everything I hoped for, the VFX were great," says the executive producer. "But the episode came to life when Joel Goldsmith added his music. Joel is a god to us and deserves much more credit than he often gets."

Though they had seen the final cut and were themselves pleased with the pilot, the producers had a lengthy wait before finding out for sure whether audiences would warm to the new show. In fact, they had written and produced ten of the twenty-episode first season before 'Rising' was finally revealed to audiences.

"I had actually said before we started shooting that anything less than a 3 rating would be disappointing," recalls Robert Cooper. "The execs thought I was insane. They were going to be ecstatic with anything over a 2.5. When the *Stargate SG-1* premiere got a 2.5 the week before, we began to get a good feeling. Some of the network and studio folks still wondered if *Stargate: Atlantis* would beat it, and truth be told they would have been happy if it had even matched *Stargate SG-1*'s popularity. The Monday after the pilot aired, we actually got something called the 'overnights' first, which are a metered reading of the major markets. That was a 3.8. We knew the actual rating usually dips from there, which it did. It ended up being a 3.2 which broke all kinds of records for the channel. It was a very, very happy day!" Å

HIDE AND SEEK

WRITTEN BY: Brad Wright and Robert C. Cooper

DIRECTED BY: David Warry•Smith

GUEST CAST: Paul McGillion (Dr Carson Beckett), Craig Veroni (Dr Peter Grodin), Christopher Heyerdahl (Halling), Reece Thompson (Jinto)

E ager to operate Ancient technology, McKay undergoes experimental treatment to activate the necessary gene. The procedure works, and he immediately activates an Ancient personal shield. Unfortunately, he soon realizes that he can't remove it. He also can't eat or drink. Meanwhile, Halling's son Jinto disappears. Power fluctuations soon begin to affect the city, and people report seeing a 'darkness' creeping around the corridors of Atlantis. Sheppard locates Jinto, who had found his way into an Ancient laboratory. The boy admits that he touched something — something that McKay identifies as a kind of 'mouse trap'. Whatever is now sucking all the energy out of Atlantis was held there and Jinto let it out. McKay thinks that the creature is pure energy, and was being researched by the Ancients as they learned to Ascend. Finally released, it's hungry and will suck all the power out of the remaining ZPMs and then move on to Atlantis' human inhabitants. Weir shuts down all the power sources she can, and Sheppard tries to return it to the trap, but the creature realizes the plan and retreats. Teyla suggests that the being might want to leave — if they activate the Stargate and provide it with an incentive, the creature may enter the wormhole. McKay rigs up a Naquada generator on a MALP, which attracts the creature to the gateroom, but the MALP's battery depletes before it can lead the creature into the open Stargate. Realizing that only he can safely enter the being's density and move the generator over the event horizon, McKay uses the personal shield and hurls the generator through the gate. The creature crosses the threshold, and although McKay's shield is sucked dry of power, he survives.

Classified Information

During filming, the episode became nick•named 'The Turtle of Power' by David Hewlett, thanks to the personal shield McKay finds and activates.

JINTO: The darkness is afraid?
TEYLA: Everything is afraid of something.

"We said from the start that the show would be as much about Atlantis as the Pegasus Galaxy," says executive producer Robert Cooper, "and we always intended the first episode after the pilot to be about the city."

After the frenetic activity of the pilot, 'Hide and Seek' gave the cast a chance to really explore their characters as individuals, and also gave the producers scope to start expanding this new galaxy beyond the boundaries of parent show *Stargate SG-1*.

"We definitely wanted to make all the characters unique from *Stargate SG-1*," agrees Cooper, though he feels that such a distinction was more natural than anything. "The fact is, as much as you try to do it on the page, when you put a living person in

Opposite: The team pulls together to solve an unusual problem.

the wardrobe and trot him out on camera, he's going to be different. People are unique. Sheppard as written was different from O'Neill and Sheppard as played by Joe Flanigan is different from Sheppard as originally written."

For Sheppard, 'Hide and Seek' was an opportunity for the character to flex his muscles in his new position of military commander of the city — a role that actor Joe Flanigan sees as probably being contrary to the major's nature: "I think he is a loner, and he's being forced to take control and lead a group of people and be less of a loner — a little less self-reliant. That requires you to trust the people that you are with, and that to a degree is the arc of the first season, until you really trust them and become a team."

McKAY: It must be a transporter.
SHEPPARD: We can name it later.

One member of the team that Sheppard did seem to have an instant rapport with was Rodney McKay. Though 'Hide and Seek' was aired first, '38 Minutes' was actually the first to be filmed, and had given the two actors a chance to work together. In doing so they had discovered a natural affinity which Flanigan feels really added to the 'shake down' process of the early season: "I think the two characters complement each other. They have two very different approaches to things. We recognized it and realized that it would be good for future episodes, and it was."

"I loved it," says David Hewlett, recalling the first time he read Cooper's script for 'Hide and Seek'. "There's nothing like throwing one of the leads off a balcony to start

MISSION ⚙ DEBRIEF
SGC

The Ancient Gene

The Ancients left behind masses of technology that was designed to be of use to them alone — activated by touch only by those carrying a gene particular to the advanced race's make-up. Humans, being direct descendents, still carry this gene in their DNA, although in most cases it is dormant. In some, however, this gene is still active, and can be used to operate Ancient technology. The first to discover this ability was Jack O'Neill of the SGC. Several members of the Atlantis expedition also have this gene, including Major John Sheppard and Dr Carson Beckett. Beckett, having researched the subject, was the first scientist to isolate the gene, and has since created an experimental therapy designed to activate the gene in humans where it is currently dormant. His first test subject, Rodney McKay, found that it worked perfectly. Having transmitted his findings back to Earth, Beckett subsequently found that his therapy was in widespread use at the SGC (see 'The Siege').

a show off — especially when it was someone else doing it and not me! I think the combination of comedy and science fiction is what makes the whole *Stargate SG-1* universe work so well. That's the kind of blend I love, where you're dealing with the Ancients' vast knowledge of superior technologies and we also get to mix it with some good comedy beats."

Of course, Ancient technology was at the heart of 'Hide and Seek', and it gave the audience the opportunity to see the arrogant McKay get his confidence knocked a little. "This is a perfect example of a man who should know better playing with things that he shouldn't. Here's this guy who knows his stuff, but is constantly battling with his own ego," says Hewlett. "It's a recurring thing for McKay. He makes stupid mistakes because he's arrogant, or he's rushing in, or he's being curious."

Of course, the saving grace for McKay's ego in 'Hide and Seek' was his self-sacrificing final act which gave the audience a glimpse of 'the real McKay' beneath his arrogant bravado.

"I always love the effects," says Hewlett of that final scene. "When you're actually doing the scene, you're thinking, 'I hope I'm going to get this right because otherwise I'm going to look really stupid!' So it's always a pleasure to see the completed thing. I think we shot the going-down-the-stairs section at the very end about four times, because as the effects progressed we realized that various things didn't relate to me properly. I saw one version, and the creature was actually a creature — it had creature-like qualities to it, you could see a head that looked at Sheppard through one of the windows. That was something that Robert Cooper, I believe, decided that no, it was an entity unlike what we had dealt with before. It's an energy creature, why should it be confined to a form familiar to us?" Å

38 MINUTES

WRITTEN BY: Brad Wright
DIRECTED BY: Mario Azzopardi

GUEST CAST: Paul McGillion (Dr Beckett), Craig Veroni (Dr Grodin), Ben Cotton (Dr Kavanagh), David Nykl (Dr Zelenka), Fiona Hogan (Simpson), Christopher Heyerdahl (Halling)

D isaster strikes when the puddle-jumper becomes wedged in the open Stargate thanks to a drive engine failing to retract. Sheppard himself is incapacitated, having encountered a leech-like creature on the planet that attached itself to his face and neck. Aboard the ship, Teyla, Ford and McKay have thirty-eight minutes to free the jumper before the gate reaches it's natural shut-off point and the wormhole closes, cutting the ship in half and exposing them all to open space. In Atlantis, Weir, Zelenka and Beckett get to work on various solutions. Trapped in the ship, McKay also works on an answer, but with the main controls already dematerialized and one engine damaged, any actions risk causing the entire ship to explode, killing the jumper crew and sending deadly debris into Stargate Control. Sheppard, meanwhile, is getting weaker. Teyla thinks that the creature has properties similar to the Wraith, and Beckett eventually realizes that the only way to save the Major may be to kill him. Using a defibrillator, Teyla and Ford stop Sheppard's heart, which causes the creature to drop off as its food source 'dies'. Although he's free of the creature, Sheppard isn't out of the woods yet — failing to resuscitate him, Teyla is forced to take the Major into the wormhole to keep him in stasis. Zelenka and McKay are eventually able to retract the drive pod, but the ship still doesn't move. Ford sends the others into the wormhole and blows the rear hatch. This forces the rest of the ship into the wormhole and back to Atlantis, where Beckett is waiting to revive Sheppard.

FORD: Why'd you close the door?
McKAY: So that when the gate shuts down and the forward section is severed, we won't be directly exposed to space.

"I wanted to do a small, character-driven episode that would help forge the team dynamic early on," says Brad Wright, of '38 Minutes'. "It helped cement the relationships, and define characters. Knocking our hero on his ass by putting a life-sucking bug on his neck and paralyzing him makes the others around him take charge and demonstrate just what they're made of. McKay may whine throughout the episode, but in the end, he does save the day."

For Joe Flanigan, who spent most of the episode with the alien 'leech' attached to his throat, it was an indication of just what he had let himself in for when he took the

Opposite: Dr Beckett prepares to revive Sheppard.

Above: Sheppard finds himself in a sticky situation.

role of Sheppard. "Now that was new," the actor laughs. "That was a crash-course in sci-fi! It was extremely uncomfortable, and Brad did it, according to him, to test my mettle! We hadn't aired yet, so I didn't know what the response was going to be, and I was sitting there on the floor of this puddle-jumper with a plastic bug wrapped around my neck, and I'm thinking to myself, 'This has got to be the worst B-movie that anyone has ever been trapped in. This is going to be incredibly stupid.' And then I saw it, and it looked great! That was another lesson for me, that I should just relax and sit back in the hands of Brad Wright and Robert Cooper, and let them do their thing. That's what I did after that, and everything got a lot easier."

Even so, during the experience, the actor reveals that he was less than happy with Sheppard's part in the episode. "No actor wants to be on his back for an entire week of shooting, just from the physical standpoint," Flanigan says with a laugh. "Then, from the creative standpoint it's not a fun position to be in, because you're stuck and you're not able to move around, the parameters are so tight. I don't enjoy stuff on my deathbed, injured soldiers and those type of scenes, so I wasn't crazy about it."

Despite his discomfort, Flanigan does admit that the episode did accomplish Wright's goals in terms of character building: "I think it was the first time that McKay and I are stuck together, and we see each other's strengths and weaknesses. I think that was the beginning of the banter between McKay and Sheppard that begins to evolve in the episodes after that."

However uncomfortable the 'plastic bug' might have been for Flanigan, it did present a hint as to where the Wraith may have first evolved from. The design of the creature itself went through several incarnations, as illustrator James Robbins explains. "The description of the bug in the first draft that we received was not all that detailed. Initially, I drew a slug-like creature about the size of a puppy with tentacles that wrapped around the victim's neck," elaborates the artist. "When I showed this to Brad, he actually did a small thumb-nail sketch of a crab-like critter that swells like an engorged tick. I took his sketch (before he almost tore it up) and developed it into the final look. I am now the proud owner of possibly the only Brad Wright *Stargate: Atlantis* drawing!"

In contrast to Flanigan's experience of the episode, Torri Higginson found it an interesting way to expand Weir's grasp of leadership: "I thought it was nice to see her making decisions, because she is the sort of leader who sits back. She's surrounded by a lot of men, but she doesn't fight for attention, doesn't demand her voice. So it was nice to have an episode where we explored her toughness, making decisions and getting on with it."

SHEPPARD: There's plenty of time to solve this thing, but you've got to stop using your mouth and start using your brain.

McKAY: Sorry. I just react to certain doom a certain way; it's a bad habit.

"One interesting thing is that the episode actually came in short after the first cut," says Brad Wright. "I had to write a couple of scenes in and shoot them second unit after the fact."

"Those are the scenes that I do with Halling and with Zelenka. Those were both afterthoughts, we shot them a few weeks later, and they are my favorite scenes in the episode," says Higginson. "Brad and I laughed about that, about the spontaneity of the writing and filming of those scenes."

For Wright, there was only one aspect of the finished episode that he in retrospect considers could have been different, and that is the episode's unusual structure. Instead of following one complete line of action, the executive producer decided to explain how Sheppard came to be in his predicament through a series of action flashbacks. "I almost regret it now," Wright confesses. "I admit, I was afraid of spending that much screen time in a confined space. If I had written the story in a more linear fashion, it might have been a very different episode." Å

SUSPICION

STORY BY: Kerry Glover
WRITTEN BY: Joseph Mallozzi
and Paul Mullie
DIRECTED BY: Mario Azzopardi

GUEST CAST: Paul McGillion (Dr Beckett), Christopher Heyerdahl (Halling), Ross Hull (Dr Corrigan), James Lafazanos (Steve)

When Sheppard and his team once again return from a scouting mission under heavy Wraith fire, Weir begins to suspect that there is a spy in the city's midst. This marks the fifth time the team has encountered the Wraith out of nine missions — clearly something is making them an easy target. Under Security Officer Bates' advice, Weir calls a meeting that excludes Teyla. Weir decides to interview each of the Athosians while closing certain areas of base operations to non-Atlantis personnel. Bates' confrontational attitude and conviction that one of the Athosians is responsible, however, does nothing to allay the Athosians' anger at being blamed for the Wraith attacks. When dry land is discovered outside Atlantis, Teyla's people decide to leave — without consulting their leader about her thoughts. Unwittingly, Teyla has been caught in the middle, and the Athosians leave her in Atlantis to make their home on the mainland. With the supposed source of the attacks removed, Weir feels it is safe to send out Sheppard's team once more, but yet again they are intercepted by the Wraith. Upon their return Bates, convinced that Teyla is deliberately giving away the team's position, orders McKay to search her possessions. Though the scientist is reluctant to comply, doing so locates the source of their problems — Teyla's locket is emitting a homing beacon transmitting on a Wraith frequency. Sheppard identifies it as the trinket he found and returned to her when they first met. Teyla is indeed the one giving away their position, but completely inadvertently. Using the device to Atlantis' advantage, Sheppard captures his first Wraith prisoner in the hope that the being — nicknamed Steve — can give them vital information.

BATES: If Colonel Sumner were still —
SHEPPARD: He's not. I am.

"When we sat down to write 'Suspicion', we had a good sense of where we wanted the characters to go," says Joseph Mallozzi, one half of the writing team that had been producing on *Stargate SG-1* since the show's fourth year. "It was almost like a pleasant change from *Stargate SG-1*, writing something different, although not that different. You're still in the familiar universe."

Still, as his writing and producing partner Paul Mullie explains, with 'Suspicion' coming so early in *Stargate: Atlantis'* first season, the writers and cast were all still learning how to work together. "It's a new show, and it's a real process when you write an

Opposite: Sheppard deals with some suspicious circumstances.

episode. You watch the dailies, and you see how the actors take it," Mullie says. "Certain types of things they will take and make better, and other things just don't work. [Then] you start writing certain types of situations for different characters, because you get a feel for that."

The episode was a pivotal moment in the development of the Atlantis community, with the inevitable issues of trust amongst two cultures thrown together through dire circumstances finally resolved. As Weir and her team found out whether their faith in Teyla had been misplaced or not, the team found themselves in interesting conflicts, all of which gave the actors opportunities to further establish their characters.

"I really enjoyed shooting 'Suspicion'," recalls Joe Flanigan, "because I really liked the storyline. To me, it was kind of a courtroom drama, and I think it was another opportunity for the character to establish himself as an unflinching leader. You realize that he can be unflinching when he believes in certain things, so it adds to the character, and it was a strong dramatic script. I was so used to doing strong dramatic material that I just felt comfortable with it."

'Suspicion' saw Sheppard taking a stand in defense of Teyla against Sergeant Bates, a marine whose hard-headed military stance continued to bring him into conflict with Atlantis team members throughout the show's first season. "I think [now], I would perhaps not take Bates so seriously," says Flanigan, "but it was important at that time, because 'Who's in charge?' became a very good question. In some ways, that episode is a bit of a power struggle."

To Flanigan, though, Sheppard's backing of Teyla and her people was less a politic move to remind his subordinates of his position and more an indication of the character's morality. "He needed to put his foot down less to establish himself as the clear

MISSION ⊕ DEBRIEF
SGC

The Athosians

The first race indigenous to the Pegasus Galaxy encountered by the human explorers from Earth, the Athosians are a peaceful, agrarian society. At one time their race had reached a significant level of technological advancement, and they still posses a few devices from this period. However, the Wraith cullings decimated their society, which now lives as a nomadic community of hunter-gatherers. Deeply spiritual, the Athosians have no divisions among themselves, with work and responsibility divided equally regardless of gender or skin color. Though forced to quit their home planet Athos due to fear of Wraith attacks, they have rebuilt their community on the mainland of the planet upon which Atlantis is situated. Though tensions have arisen between the two societies, these have been resolved, and the Athosians are always willing to offer help and advice to Weir and her team.

Above: Teyla Emmagen faces
problems as the Athosians
integrate into Atlantis.

military superior and more because he believed what was happening was wrong and
that Teyla was in fact a great asset. Secondarily, it would solidify his position as the
military leader."

"It was a difficult one, because she felt very in the middle," says Torri Higginson of
Weir's reaction to the conflict. "So she brought in Bates, and allowed him to do the
hard-ball stuff. I think she wished that he wasn't as hard-ball as he was, but she recognized at that point that it would be good to have that balance, because Sheppard was
not going to go that way at all. There was something very diplomatic about her going,
'I'll bring in another guy to do that.'"

STEVE: When I'm free, you'll be the first I feed upon.
SHEPPARD: Okey-dokey. I'll go make myself a sandwich.

While 'Suspicion' served to cement Teyla as a trustworthy ally, it saw the Athosians
as a whole leave Atlantis to begin a new life on the mainland, something that
Christopher Heyerdahl had been expecting for his character Halling for some time. "It
was something that had been talked about, because of the simple reality of who Teyla
was," he explains. "She is somebody who is incredibly strong, curious, a searcher. It was
only natural that she would become involved with saving the universe. She was going to
be the one that would be a part of the new Atlantis. So who then was going to lead the
people? Halling seemed the natural choice for that."

Though he hadn't known quite how this move would be accomplished, Heyerdahl
very much enjoyed the way 'Suspicion' set up the Athosians' move. "These people were
taken out of their home — they were masters of themselves not less than a few months
before, and now suddenly they are being second-guessed and every decision is made by
these strangers. From Halling's point of view, that had to change. Where is the pride in
a free people if they have to ask for everything? So it was actually quite exciting to see
them move to the land again, where they could hunt, grow, and be as free as possible
under the circumstances." Å

CHILDHOOD'S END

WRITTEN BY: Martin Gero
DIRECTED BY: David Winning

GUEST CAST: Courtenay J. Stevens (Keras), Dominic Zamprogna (Aries), Shane Meier (Neleus)

Detecting a power source on an apparently uninhabited planet, the puddle-jumper goes to investigate but is forced to land when the engine fails. None of the team's equipment is working, and Sheppard, Teyla, Ford and McKay find themselves surrounded by armed children. They are introduced to Keras, the children's 'senior' elder, who is also incredibly young. In fact, the population practices ritual self-sacrifice on their twenty-fifth birthday, believing it a protection from the Wraith. They also have a Wraith skeleton that 'fell out of the sky' centuries ago. Aries, Keras' imminent successor, wants the team to leave immediately, but Keras enjoys talking to Sheppard. McKay uses the time to locate the power source — a ZPM. The device generates an electromagnetic field so no technology works there. The Wraith can't detect them and therefore don't visit the planet. McKay persuades Sheppard to let him take the ZPM back to Atlantis and see how much power it has, but deactivating the shield unwittingly triggers a homing device on the Wraith skeleton. McKay discovers that the ZPM doesn't have enough power to be of use to Atlantis — and formulates a theory of how the ritual suicide started. The shield generated is only strong enough to protect a small area, so the sacrifice is a brutal form of population control. Meanwhile, tempers flare between Keras and Aries, who is convinced that the 'full growns' presence will attract the Wraith. Sheppard, seeing the Wraith signal, realizes that they can't leave until the children are protected again. A tense stand-off follows until McKay manages to replace the ZPM, with eyewitnesses seeing the shield's power. Sheppard and his team leave peacefully, vowing to return to check on the flourishing civilization.

McKAY: Didn't fly over this on the way down, did we?
SHEPPARD: I don't know. I was kind of busy with the whole trying not to get us killed thing.

'Childhood's End' marked the entrance of new writer Martin Gero, who with this script would pave the way to becoming a key element in *Stargate: Atlantis'* writing and producing team. Gero, a serious fan of science fiction, being familiar with parent show *Stargate SG-1*, was immediately interested in becoming involved with this fledgling new series.

"They put the word out for freelancers, and asked me to pitch based solely off the pilot script," the writer explains. "That was the only thing that existed. No one had

Opposite: McKay makes some new friends.

Above: One of the many moral dilemmas faced by the Atlantis team.

been cast, there weren't any sets built, they had nothing to show except for the script. So I read the script and came up with a couple of pitches, and one of them was 'Childhood's End'. The thing is that writers never work alone on a show like this. I just came up with a core idea of a planet of children that had established this ritualistic suicide pact in order to — as they thought — preserve themselves from the Wraith. And with *Stargate: Atlantis*, one of the big mandates was that it had to be a bit darker than *Stargate SG-1*, so that story fit right in. Thankfully I did an okay job on it and got hired!"

"Ah yes, the 'bratlet' episode," recalls David Hewlett with a laugh. "That was actually a tough shoot. We were out on location and there were kids hanging from every tree! The kids were probably better behaved than most of us, but it was just a technically difficult shoot. There's [also] a danger of a planet of children turning into — dare I offend people — the Ewok village, with lots of singing and cute little animals. [But] those kids were so cute, and they were really good — they hit their marks, they knew their lines, they were really well behaved... Perhaps a little less respectful towards me than I felt they should be," he muses, "but they were fantastic!"

Though Hewlett may have found working with his young cast mates fun, for McKay it put him in yet another unexpected — and funny — situation. "I find myself cackling at some of those scenes," Hewlett says of the finished episode. "McKay doesn't seem like the sort of person who would like children. It's everything that he doesn't want. I think he would like a girlfriend, perhaps, but it's all science for him. If Zelenka was a woman, maybe that could work out," he says with a laugh. "But even that would get in the way of his sad little scientific existence!"

For Joe Flanigan, initial concerns about the overall tone and direction of the episode went a little deeper than worries about working with children. "I remember approaching Brad [Wright] and telling him, 'This script doesn't work because there's no real threat,'" Flanigan recalls, "and he said 'Yeah, there is. These kids are going to kill themselves.' I said, 'Well that's not a threat to *us*.' And then he said 'It's a threat because you care.' It was a really important point to make, because there was no physical threat — for the most part it was minor, a bunch of kids with bows and arrows. But it is character exploration, it's seeing how much they care, and it reveals that Sheppard has a softer side to him."

'Childhood's End' was also an interesting interlude for Elizabeth Weir, as her moral compass was challenged by the discovery of the children's functioning ZPM. Should Atlantis take what they need though it's not theirs, simply with the argument that the population could be brought back to the city for protection?

"I remember being frustrated," says Torri Higginson, "because I wanted to say more. That was something that she really would have fought against. But that happens, there are stories that have to be told, and it's hard to appease every character — but to be honest, I felt there was a bit of inconsistency there."

'Childhood's End' marked the first instance where Weir was faced with the possibility of compromising on her strict moral standing, as life in the Pegasus Galaxy forces them all to adapt. For the actress, it is interesting — although also somewhat painful — to see the character change under such pressures.

CRSTR: You're mean.
McKRY: Thank you for finally noticing.

"She's definitely a different person," Higginson says of Weir's sojourn in Atlantis. "I think she was probably a very irritating person in her twenties, because she just lived very much by her political ideals, and the idea that compromise was something that was comparable to weakness as far as your moral thoughts go. We are dealing with different worlds here, and no matter how much I still think she would have fought, it is forcing her to make huge compromises that I think will cost her. Some of them I think have made us better people, have made us learn a different level of openness and humility, and other choices have scarred us a bit. I think every character has a few episodes where they have made decisions that they might have changed given the chance."

"I'll be honest, it's the least favorite of my own episodes," confesses Martin Gero, "for a number of reasons. The episode came in really long — it was nine minutes over, which meant that a lot of the humor had to be cut out. That made it more somber and drier than it was ever intended to be. I think act five goes on too long and the stand-off is a little too long, things like that. But those were hard lessons that I learned and have never made again!" Å

POISONING THE WELL

WRITTEN BY: Mary Kaiser
TELEPLAY BY: Damian Kindler
DIRECTED BY: Brad Turner

GUEST CAST: Paul McGillion (Dr Beckett), Alan Scarfe (Chancellor Druhin), Allison Hossack (Perna)

Atlantis meets the Hoffan, a society that has been developing a 'vaccine' against the Wraith for generations. Beckett reluctantly agrees to assist their leading scientist, Perna, in trying to complete their research. Beckett soon realizes that they really are close to an answer, and Earth's advanced technology could be the key to completion before the Wraith attack again. By testing their new results on cells garnered during an attack years before, the results prove that they are on the brink of a breakthrough. However, they need to test the vaccine on fresher cells — using Atlantis' Wraith prisoner and a willing human subject. Weir is disgusted at the thought, but is convinced by Sheppard that they have no other option. 'Steve' is given the chance to feed upon a terminally ill man, a volunteer who has taken the serum. The vaccine seems an immediate success, and Steve is unable to feed. Overjoyed, the Hoffan's government wants to rush ahead and begin planet-wide vaccinations, but Beckett urges caution and more research. Matters are complicated when Steve dies of massive organ failure and the post-mortem shows this was caused by absorption of the vaccine. Sheppard is worried that when the Wraith discover this, they'll wipe the Hoffan out. Then Perna reports that their Hoffan test subject has also died. Beckett is convinced that the serum is to blame, but the government presses ahead with widespread inoculations. Soon, half the population is dying of the same complaint — Perna being one of them. Horrified, Beckett tries to get the Hoffan to stop, but a planetary vote has been taken and the vaccinations will continue. They deem that half their population is worth the sacrifice for 'freedom' from the Wraith.

BECKETT: This isn't about making mistakes, Perna. This is about the end justifying the means, and in our profession that's a very slippery slope.

"The story originally came from a writer named Mary Kaiser, who pitched an idea about a society whose answer to stopping the cullings is to invent an anti-Wraith drug," says supervising producer Damian Kindler, who penned the screenplay for this episode. "From there, Brad and Rob spun the story a bit further until they had a great premise, which was that these people had been working on this drug for generations and the results were still not right. That gave the Atlantis team a great door in, as they decide to help perfect it. It became clear that this wasn't going to be a typical mystery/action/intrigue type episode. It was about a search for answers that leads to

Opposite: Dr Beckett examines the Hoffan's vaccine research.

a moral question about the price people are willing to pay for security and peace of mind; quite relevant in today's political climate, I think."

Though primarily employed on *Stargate SG-1*, Kindler was very happy to turn his hand to polishing 'Poisoning the Well'. "Ultimately, the decision was made to have the script written in house, mainly in light of the fact that tone was a key factor in making this story work," the producer explains. "I was incredibly honored that Brad asked me to jump in and write for the new show."

SHEPPARD: You guys do have names, right? Let me guess... Steve?
WRAITH: I am your death! That is all you need to know.
SHEPPARD: I prefer Steve.

The writer reports that he had great fun writing for the new cast, in particular Paul McGillion's recurring character Carson Beckett, who found himself at the centre of the story. "Writing Beckett was easily the most pleasurable aspect of writing the script," Kindler recalls. "I could always hear his voice in my head, he was that familiar to me. I'm half Scottish on my mother's side and my dad's a doctor, so in a way I was accessing my mum's 'Scottishness' while also turning to my dad for all sorts of help with the medical research side of the story. It was amazing to be able to learn obscure Scottish expressions and also get a fount of medical knowledge all in one phone call to my parents," he says. "Also, I have to credit Paul McGillion with inspir-

MISSION ⊕ DEBRIEF
SGC

The Wraith

The Wraith are an extremely powerful and rapacious predator, able to survive in hibernation for thousands of years and even in the harshest conditions — including being able to recover from grave injury — providing they feed regularly. This is accomplished by means of invasive feeding tubes in the hands, which attach to a homo sapien's chest area to drain its 'life-force'. It is possible that it was this process that enabled the Wraith to evolve from non-sentient creatures (as seen in the episode '38 Minutes') to the highly evolved and technologically advanced species they now are. It is also possible that this process of absorption could be their downfall. Following the death of 'Steve' after he ingested particles of the Hoffan's vaccine, Dr Beckett surmised that the serum fused with the chemical the Wraith use to facilitate feeding, forming a lethal toxin. Though such information is not currently of use, in future it may prove invaluable.

Above: Sheppard and Teyla try to understand the Hoffan.

ing me as well. He's such a terrific guy and very soon after meeting him, I knew that his talent and dedication to the role would shine through whatever I gave him. The pressure was to make the script as strong as his work ethic."

'Poisoning the Well' is a dark interlude for the Atlantis team, as they discover just how far they are from home not only physically but also ethically. "I think deciding to use a human to test the serum was one of the defining moments in the episode," says Kindler. "Everyone who read the pilot knew that *Stargate: Atlantis* was going to be a darker series than *Stargate SG-1*. Our heroes are cut off from Earth, facing overwhelming odds against a formidable enemy. Therefore the stakes are higher on an episode-by-episode basis, thus the decisions our heroes make will be difficult ones from time to time. That, to me, is one of the things that makes *Stargate: Atlantis* such a cool show. It can go darker and examine ethical shades of grey, and you don't feel it's a left turn from the normal tone of the series. I think 'Poisoning the Well' showed early on in the inaugural season just how heavy and dramatic *Stargate: Atlantis* can be. Have our heroes crossed a moral line? I don't think so. But the stakes at hand do mean that line is constantly moving."

The audience also learns that the simple fact may be that the Wraith are unable to feed on anything other than a human life-force, making it difficult to find a peaceful solution to the threat of their existence. "A bad guy that can satisfy itself on the life-force of a cow or chicken does not inspire the same kind of dread as one that only feeds on humans," Kindler points out, "so it was a no-brainer to make the Wraith dependant on humans to live. And the fact that there are so many Wraith spread across the Pegasus Galaxy makes 'wiping them out' an insurmountable challenge. One of the issues 'Poisoning the Well' brings up is that if we can understand what makes a Wraith a Wraith physiologically, we may have a chance at better defending ourselves from them, if not potentially hobbling them *en masse* at some point down the line." Å

UNDERGROUND

WRITTEN BY: Peter DeLuise
DIRECTED BY: Brad Turner

GUEST CAST: Colm Meaney (Cowen), Ari Cohen (Tyrus),
Erin Chambers (Sora), Craig Veroni (Dr Grodin)

Atlantis is running low on food supplies, so Teyla offers to introduce them to the Genii, a shy pre-industrial race who have traded fairly with the Athosians for decades. However, the Genii turn out to be less willing to trade as fairly with Sheppard as with Teyla. Besides the offered medicines, the Genii want a supply of C4, which they say will be used for clearing arable land. Sheppard goes back to Atlantis with McKay to explain this to Weir, who is less than happy with the prospect of becoming an arms dealer. However, there isn't a lot she can do since Sheppard has already agreed to the deal. On their way back to the Genii village, Sheppard and McKay make an astounding discovery — an underground bunker where the Genii appear to be building a nuclear weapon. The Genii, far from the backward peasants they purport to be, are a highly industrialized underground society, building an atomic bomb that they plan to use on the sleeping Wraith ships with the help of a Wraith data device gathered during the last culling. Unfortunately, thanks to Sheppard the Wraith are waking up and it may be too late. Angered by this, the Genii force Sheppard's team to engage in an information gathering mission aboard a Wraith ship that has not yet stirred, which goes according to plan until the Wraith sense their presence and one of the Genii is killed. Returning to the Genii planet, Cowen holds Sheppard responsible for the loss and tries to take the team's puddle-jumper by force. However, Sheppard has come prepared and de-cloaks two other ships, forcing the Genii to stand down so they can leave. Atlantis has made another enemy.

COWEN: You do not want to make an enemy of the Genii.
SHEPPARD: You know what? Same here.

"When I wrote 'Underground', it was the first script to be turned in after the pilot," writer/producer Peter DeLuise reveals. "The problem with that is that all we knew was what we read in the pilot script. Obviously, what's wrong with that is when they actually went to cast it the characters changed. For example, David Hewlett's character was not originally one of the characters on the show. The original scientist character was supposed to be someone else, a different character, and when it was determined that nobody was quite good enough for that particular role and that David was standing by and had history from the previous show, it just seemed like a naturally smart move to have him be the guy. Plus, we had established

Opposite: Sheppard and McKay prepare to go underground.

Above: Teyla and Lieutenant Ford discover a dark underside to the Genii.

that this character — after Carter — was pretty much the smartest guy when it came to Wormhole Theory. So that was also a natural as well. And the fact that he was a fantastic actor and very professional didn't hurt either!"

As a result, the natural thing for the writers to do was focus on the one character they had experience with. "David was the only person we actually knew how to write for. We knew about his dry scathing wit and his ability to be very funny with lines that were potentially not funny. We could write lines for him and feel comfortable that he would be able to pull it off, whereas the other characters were unknown. Everyone except for Weir, who had been on *Stargate SG-1*. In her case, we understood the character. We knew what the character would say but not necessarily how she would say it because Torri was coming in to take over the role. So all those things contributed to making it very difficult to write the characters effectively early on."

Because of this, DeLuise found himself revising the script again once the pilot had been filmed, to make sure that the right lines were going to the right characters. "I wrote most of the jokes for the character of Sheppard," he explains. "Because I had very few guidelines for 'Underground', I wrote a lot of jokes for Sheppard that sounded exactly like something O'Neill would say. I just used him as a kind of indicator of what we were going for. Then they cast David Hewlett. McKay and Sheppard have a lot of scenes together, they go walking off and find the special entrance to the underground. In all those scenes, I couldn't have both of them being very silly. Not everybody can be funny in the scene! If there's supposed to be some sort of perceived danger and everybody's cracking jokes then the suspension of disbelief is lost. The audience will think, 'Well, the characters don't seem to be worried because they're all cracking jokes, so why should the audience be worried?' So somebody has to take the situation seriously. That means you can't have everybody making silly jokes all the time. So a lot of the jokes that I originally wrote for Sheppard ended up being jokes that David Hewlett delivered. That was a major contributing factor to the scripts changing and also in us feeling out what the characters would be."

Sheppard: As far as your secret down here goes… McKay: …We say: what secret, giant, underground bunker?

'Underground' was a significant episode of the first season, because it introduced the Atlanteans' second major enemy — the Genii. "Brad Wright always knew that he wanted a race of human beings that we would be at odds with, that we would have some sort of political struggle with," explains DeLuise. "And at first all the indicators were that the Genii were in essence the Pegasus Galaxy's version of the Tok'ra. There was this underground organization that was devoted to rebelling against the oppression of the Wraith, and to me it felt a lot like the Tok'ra, so I used them as an example. But the big twist at the end is that these people are not that friendly! In fact they hold quite the grudge, and they are offended by us waking the Wraith ahead of schedule. That is a reoccurring theme on *Stargate: Atlantis*, because it helps us stay culpable. Because we woke the Wraith up early, we have a responsibility to the people that have been making plans to try to thwart the Wraith the next time they are going to attack. They are going to be attacked ahead of schedule, and it's our fault, so we have to try and help them. That is a reoccurring theme, and it gives us permission to get involved instead of just saying 'Oh, sorry, we screwed it up, sorry.'"

Having started on *Stargate SG-1* as a director, the hardest part of turning in his script for *Stargate: Atlantis* was handing it over to be filmed by someone else. "From what the writing staff has indicated to me, that is pretty much par for the course. You always feel that it could have been done differently or that what you had in mind was slightly different," DeLuise admits. "But I tell you, Brad Turner is such a great director that once I saw what he had done with the episode, I was really pleased. I don't always say that for every script that I've written that has been directed by other people. But Brad Turner is a very talented director." Å

HOME

WRITTEN BY: Joseph Mallozzi
and Paul Mullie
DIRECTED BY: Holly Dale

GUEST CAST: Don S. Davis (General Hammond),
Garwin Sanford (Simon)

Sheppard's team finds an apparently uninhabited planet shrouded in mist, which carries an intense form of energy — an energy that could be enough to power a wormhole back to Earth. McKay believes that by using the control crystal in the Atlantis Stargate and channeling the energy in the atmosphere into the gate, they will be able to open the gate back to the SGC. Since they don't know if Earth has found another ZPM, it will likely be a one-way trip. Weir gives the go-ahead to send a radio signal, but when they establish contact, the SGC tells them that the Asgard have helped them develop the Prometheus' hyperdrive engines, so much so that if they come home they will be able to return to Atlantis by ship in about a month. The team returns to Earth, taking Teyla along, where General Hammond tells Weir that he is in favor of abandoning the Pegasus Galaxy altogether in light of the Wraith threat. Troubled, Weir goes to visit her partner Simon while Sheppard shows Teyla Earth. Things soon seem to be going wrong — Hammond tells them that they now can't return to Atlantis, Ford finds himself reassigned, and Sheppard discovers that two of his best friends have returned from the dead. As they realize that something is very wrong, Hammond reveals himself to be an alien from the planet. His is a race that exist as energy, and they have developed this 'reality' as a way of preventing the team from using the Stargate, which is fatal to them. Discovering this, Weir uses her skill as a diplomat to affect their release, with the understanding that they will never return.

FORD: I've never seen so much nothing.
SHEPPARD: And I've never walked so far to see it.

"When I saw the set, I thought, 'This is great!'" Joe Flanigan says with a laugh, recalling Sheppard's fantasy bachelor pad. "It was better than I expected! I was thinking, 'Okay, we got girls, beer, pizza — what else do we need?' For people that probably didn't notice, I'm a big Johnny Cash fan, and we stuck a Johnny Cash poster up on the wall, which is really the tip-off to Sheppard that this is in fact an illusion."

Having spent six months in the science fiction genre, Flanigan, the veteran drama star, was pleased to get the opportunity to go 'home'. "I was initially excited to do 'Home'," he says, "because I thought going back to Earth would be kind of exciting. And then I realized that space is more exciting," Flanigan laughs again. "After looking at 'Home', I thought, 'Damn, we're so less *heroic* on Earth. Get us back into space!'"

Opposite: 'General
Hammond' reveals his
true nature.

For Weir, the visit to Earth was less comfortable, as she found herself suddenly and permanently divorced from Atlantis. Though they so far had not been realized, 'Home' did reveal some of Weir's deepest fears regarding the tenuous nature of her position as leader if the military ever decide that Atlantis should be a purely military base, which Higginson feels is central to her character's personal philosophy and beliefs.

WEIR: Rodney, what you need to do is just calm down.
McKAY: No, what I need to do is get very agitated because all of this is a *lie*!

"It's about Atlantis not being America's 'manifest destiny'," the actress explains. "That is her concern, and that was her concern when she was on Earth and involved in diplomatic relations. I don't know how much the producers like to hear me say this, but it's interesting as far as politics goes nowadays! Joe [Flanigan] and I enjoy talking about what's going on in America, about the idea of taking over and what that means. I think Weir is very much against that, and is saying, 'This is an *Earth* project. It's about bringing cultures together, and the more we can understand about ourselves as human beings both on this planet and other planets, then the better human beings we can be. The more we can discover about other cultures through friendship and through sharing of knowledge, not through power over them, then, again, the better human beings we can be and the more chance of peace we have.' So I think that has always been her concern about it becoming a strictly military mission."

MISSION (Å) DEBRIEF
SGC

Zero Point Modules

Among their other technologies, the Ancients devised a clean and virtually inexhaustible power source named a Zero Point Module, or ZPM for short. Used to power most of their larger devices, they developed the ZPMs from 'vacuum energy', derived from an enclosed area of sub-space time. Having used Earth's only ZPM to power the Stargate that took the Atlantis expedition to Pegasus, the team are unable to return home again unless they can find another to power the Atlantis Stargate, since it takes a huge amount of energy to open a wormhole from one galaxy to another. The city of Atlantis itself also runs on ZPMs, though having been used to hold the city's underwater shield in place for 10,000 years, two of the three have been depleted and the third is waning. Though the team has rigged Naquada generators into the Ancient technology to take some of the stress from the last ZPM, it is vital that the team locate more as soon as possible, both to activate Atlantis' protective shield again and so that they can visit Earth with ease.

'Home' also gave Higginson a chance to explore how Weir is dealing with the necessary isolation of leadership in the Pegasus Galaxy by giving her an emotional, if short-lived, 'reunion' with her partner Simon. "I think for her it's lonelier than anyone else, because she doesn't have the bonding of the group. She realizes that she can't be one of the buddies, she's already, as a woman and as a non-military woman, struggling for control and that's a struggle on a daily basis. If you're the leader no matter what, even if you're a male General, there has to be a separation from the people that you are in charge of. And for her there's even more of one. I think she fights against it, and that's where some of her weaknesses come from. I think she crosses lines sometimes that undermine her power because she does want to be humane and personable, and she is very lonely."

For veteran writer/producers Joseph Mallozzi and Paul Mullie, the challenge in writing 'Home' came as a result of the episode's original intended destination, which was not the Pegasus Galaxy at all! "The original pitch for the story was actually a *Stargate SG-1* idea," explains Mallozzi. "It was around last year, but we ended up using it for *Stargate: Atlantis*." Adds Mullie with a dry laugh, "As we've often said, when you've done this much television and this many seasons, all the ideas that got rejected earlier on get used."

Though 'Home' may not have worked as well for *Stargate SG-1*, once moved to the *Stargate: Atlantis* arena the episode became the perfect opportunity to stage the return of the much-loved General Hammond, played by *Stargate SG-1* favorite Don S. Davis, as well as an interesting opportunity to further flesh out the characters' backgrounds. Å

Classified Information

The scene in which Weir visits Simon was actually written for 'Rising', but because of time constraints was inserted into and filmed for 'Home' instead.

THE STORM

STORY BY: Jill Blotevogel
WRITTEN BY: Martin Gero
DIRECTED BY: Martin Wood

GUEST CAST: Colm Meaney (Cowen), Erin Chambers (Sora), Robert Davi (Commander Acastus Kolya), Ryan Robbins (Ladon), Paul McGillion (Dr Carson Beckett), Michael Puttonen (Smeadon)

Sheppard and Ford discover a massive storm heading for Atlantis and the Athosian settlement. Many miles across, its destructive force is huge and the city is in imminent danger. As McKay and Zelenka struggle to find a way of protecting the city without the power needed to activate Atlantis' shield, Weir urges Sheppard to find somewhere that they can evacuate to until the storm has passed. Sheppard visits the Manarians, who eventually agree to take in the refugees. Returning to the city to deliver the news, Sheppard discovers that McKay and Zelenka have something of a plan. If they can disengage the grounding stations that protect Atlantis from lightning, they may be able to channel that energy to power Atlantis' massive shield. Disabling the grounding stations, however, will result in the city's corridors being electrified, so the population must evacuate anyway, apart from a skeleton crew. On the mainland, Teyla, Beckett and Ford find themselves trapped whilst waiting to evacuate the last Athosians and are forced to wait out the weather in their puddle-jumper. Meanwhile, the Manarians have informed the Genii that Atlantis and its supplies will be theirs for the taking during the storm. While Sheppard battles through the weather to release one of the needed grounding stations, Commander Kolya and a strike team take the control room, along with Weir and McKay. Hearing events over his radio, Sheppard does what he can to sabotage Kolya's plans, killing the soldiers that the commander sends to eliminate him and warning Kolya that he will do worse unless the Genii leave. Kolya, however, has Weir and McKay — and isn't afraid to use them as bargaining chips, preparing to kill Elizabeth as payback for the deaths of his men.

FORD: How could something as big as Atlantis just sink? SHEPPARD: I'm sure the passengers on the *Titanic* were asking themselves the same question.

"I handed 'Childhood's End' in on a Wednesday, and got a call on Thursday morning from Brad and Robert, who said, 'Great, we love it, you're hired, be here next Monday,'" recalls Martin Gero with a laugh. "I was living in Toronto at the time, and had to drop everything. I arrived in Vancouver at around 1.30pm on Monday, and the transport guys picked me up and I said, 'So, are we going to the hotel?' and they're like, 'No, no, they want you at the office right away'! So I came into my office with my three big bags of everything I owned, and everyone was very nice and said,

Opposite: Ford and Beckett don't like the look of that sky.

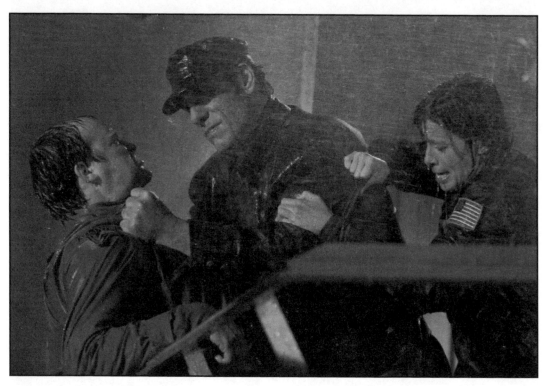

Above: Guest star Robert Davi shows the *Atlantis* cast his acting moves.

'Welcome aboard, would you like some water? So what's next?'" Gero laughs again, "I pitched out a story that I think everyone can agree was terrible, and there was that fear in everyone's eyes, as if they were thinking 'Was this a mistake? Has he signed his contract yet?' Brad Wright said, 'Well, we just bought this story from Jill Blotevogel.' Basically the only thing we kept from the original story was Atlantis getting stuck in a storm. And he said, 'We're thinking of taking the bad guys in 'Underground' and turning them into a regular bad guy for us. So how do you feel about writing a two-parter about Atlantis running into a storm and the Genii storming the base at our moment of weakness?' He pretended like I had a choice in the matter!"

Stepping in to direct was Martin Wood on his second foray into the Pegasus Galaxy after directing 'Rising'. Though he had, in conjunction with the executive producers, been keeping a close eye on proceedings as the season progressed, 'The Storm' marked his return to the *Stargate: Atlantis* sets for real — and what a return it was. For a start, Atlantis was to be flooded, and much of the action would have to be filmed in the pouring rain.

"A lot of my time was spent figuring out the logistics of how to get that to work. For the most part, the action part of the story was familiar, but that rain part was not

— and that was really fun! We got [special effects supervisor] Wray Douglas in there, and Bridget McGuire created a set that was waterproof. Originally what was supposed to happen was, we went out in the rain and then when the power went down, McKay goes over to Kolya and says, 'Can we go and stay in the shelter?' But I walked into Brad's office and said, 'Absolutely not. Kolya's not going anywhere they're not. Let's not have shelter.' So the set was actually created not to have an overhang. So no matter where you went on the set, you were going to get wet."

"God, it was cold," laughs Torri Higginson. "David and I laughed about it at the time — of course they shot it before the hiatus, so we could get really sick and spend the next three weeks in bed! Martin was very funny because he kept warning us, 'It's not going to be very comfortable.' On the day, he went in to test the water himself. He stood there and let himself get soaked, and then he came out and said, 'It's going to really suck.' They had huge jet fans blowing fire hoses of water at us! It hurt, and your eyes were stinging — but it's fun, I like that. In a way you don't have to act, you're just responding."

McKAY: I will try, but despite what you all may think, I am not Superman.
SHEPPARD: Was anyone seriously thinking that?

For Higginson, whose career to date had included plenty of action, the three days she spent filming in the water for 'The Storm' represented the most action-oriented opportunity she had had as Weir. "It all happened so fast, it wasn't something they ever considered happening, which was short sighted of them," says the actress, thinking of Weir's reaction to the danger she found herself in. "They should have perhaps had some failsafe. It happened so quickly that there wasn't time to think about, 'Well, how is she going to respond?' She's all of a sudden just responding to it, and the only tool she has is her mouth. That really is all she has. And that was difficult too, because there were these scenes where she was trying to reason with Kolya and talk to him, but I had to scream it because of the rain. Which was really difficult, because I thought, 'Well, now I can't use connection.' You want to just be quiet and look somebody in the eye — that's how you want to meet with somebody. Screaming at somebody goes against the feeling of diplomacy. So that was a challenge."

"I think it's a bit like childbirth, where you forget the pain because otherwise people would only have one child," David Hewlett laughs. "I can't help looking back fondly on that, because I'm sure it was hell, absolute hell, and I'm sure I made everyone's life a misery *because* it was hell, but it just looks so damn cool! There's just nothing like that. I've never experienced that before. I've done rain tower stuff before and it's cold, but when you start firing water from giant fans and having gallons of it running down your back, it's something else." Å

THE EYE

WRITTEN BY: Martin Gero
DIRECTED BY: Martin Wood

GUEST CAST: Erin Chambers (Sora), Don Ackerman (Doran), Robert Davi (Commander Acastus Kolya), Paul McGillion (Dr Carson Beckett), Ryan Robbins (Ladon)

McKay convinces Kolya that he needs both of them alive if he wants the city in one piece, as McKay still has to execute his plan to raise the shield, for which he needs Weir's access codes. Kolya, however, tells Sheppard that he has shot Weir dead. As McKay works, Sheppard begins to wage a war of sabotage against Kolya's team by disabling Atlantis' generators. He is determined that Atlantis will be destroyed rather than fall into Genii hands, and when Kolya calls for reinforcements, Sheppard manages to raise the Stargate's shield, wiping out all but five of the sixty men en route. Angered, Kolya contacts Sheppard and tells him that Weir is alive, and unless he restores the generators immediately, both she and McKay will die, and Atlantis will be destroyed by the storm. Meanwhile, the eye of the storm has passed over the mainland, giving Teyla, Ford and Beckett enough time to take off and head for the city to help Sheppard, who is now trying to replace the generators. With the generators returned and Sheppard reunited with his team, McKay fakes Kolya out by telling the commander that his plan has failed. Kolya, though, decides to take Weir and McKay with him as the Genii evacuate, determined that the humans should be punished. Sheppard stops Kolya taking Weir by shooting him in the shoulder but elsewhere, Teyla is engaged in a fierce fight with Kolya's lieutenant, Sora, who still blames the Athosian for her father's death. The two women just make it into the control room with Beckett in time for McKay to activate the shield and save Atlantis from a massive tidal wave.

KOLYA: If the power is not restored to generator three in the next ten minutes, Dr Weir dies.
SHEPPARD: Again, you mean.

Having put the cast of *Stargate: Atlantis* through the wringer in 'The Storm', writer Martin Gero and director Martin Wood cranked up the action to dry them off in 'The Eye'. "At the time we shot that, it was as good as we had gotten. I thought that was by far our best episode," says Joe Flanigan, of the mid-season two-parter. "Those were fun. My favorite episodes are the big action episodes. I like big physical action, I like fights, I like being rained on and I like shooting — I'm very, very adolescent when it comes to those things! 'The Storm'/'The Eye' fulfilled all of that. I got to shoot big guns and do stunts and fight."

Flanigan also appreciated the episode for the return of the Genii, which the actor

Opposite: Sheppard turns saboteur to protect Atlantis.

sees as one of the most successful aspects of *Stargate: Atlantis'* first season. "I think one of the best storylines that we have is that we have come into this place and awakened the Wraith. All these people were really happy — they were going along nice and quietly until we showed up and started sticking our noses in. It's a great place to start from, which is that we're always going to be in trouble. When we first started out, Brad and I discussed introducing a true nemesis, a real arch-enemy, not alien but of the human variety that could really go toe-to-toe on a lot of different issues as opposed to simply wanting to eat us. I was afraid to have [Sheppard's] enemies continually alien-like, because I just thought to myself, 'Well, of course you're scared of them — who wouldn't be?' I thought it might be more interesting if there was a real opponent that was human."

This 'arch-enemy' appeared in the form of heavyweight guest star Robert Davi as Genii military commander Acastus Kolya. "Well, talking about storms," says David Hewlett with a dry chuckle, "Robert Davi is one of those actors who loves spontaneity, so he's always got you on edge. I've always had this theory that the stuff that is hardest to shoot is the best to watch, because you can get comfortable and that takes the edge off your performance. And with Robert Davi — frankly the guy can be pretty scary! He's very intense about everything, and he's playing an evil guy. But he doesn't want to play it on just one note, so it's really varied. It keeps you on your toes because you don't know where he's going to go. He'll get a gleam in his eye and he'll try something. I find McKay generally becomes very still around Robert Davi because I don't want to draw attention to myself!"

MISSION (A) DEBRIEF
SGC

The Genii

A technologically advanced race, the Genii have resorted to disguising their true selves by moving their civilization underground, where they exist in vast tunnels to avoid the Wraith. Above ground, they seem to their neighboring planets as nothing more than simple farmers. Their entire society revolves around the desire to see the Wraith destroyed, and they feel that they can accomplish this by detonating an atom bomb while the Wraith sleep. Being completely dedicated to this mission makes the Genii uncompromising and unforgiving of the Wraith, making enemies of anyone who delays their plan. The Genii, instead of joining forces with the new Atlanteans, attempted to take the city for themselves. When this failed, they continued their assaults on Weir's people, in the hope of gaining some advantage over the Wraith from the information gathered by Sheppard and his team.

Above: Sora puts Teyla through her paces.

"He's a scary dude on camera," agrees Martin Gero, who was delighted with Davi's performance. "He's got a menacing physical presence. I mean, in real life he's one of the sweetest guys around, and to have him be so jovial and happy [and then] have him be this dread embodiment of menace is a funny juxtaposition. We totally lucked out with the casting of that role."

McKAY: Did you ever doubt me?
WEIR: Yes, several times.

'The Eye' also featured high-octane roles for Dr Beckett, Lieutenant Ford and Teyla, without whom the Genii would have overrun Atlantis entirely. For Paul McGillion in particular, 'The Eye' illustrated what an unexpected turn his character had taken by this point in the season: "Sometimes he's the cowardly lion, sometimes he's a reluctant hero — he's a neat character because he gets to do all these things. That was a great opportunity for myself, Rainbow and Rachel to have some camaraderie and for Beckett to make some moral decisions about whether or not to go and fly the puddle-jumper and be a committed player."

The 'b' story of Ford, Beckett and Teyla trying to get back to Atlantis also provided an important extra element to the finished episode. "'The Eye' was a minute and a half under, which actually turned out to be a blessing in disguise," the writer explains. "Originally Ford, Teyla and Beckett find Sheppard right away. They choose the right generator station. We did it because we thought we were running long, but I always thought, 'God, it's so coincidental.' So when we were under, I walked into Brad's office and said, 'I would love to go in and complicate them finding Sheppard. It's a great opportunity for us to do that.' So we basically did another day of shooting with them arming up and choosing the wrong generator and going to the transporter. It's great because it amps up the tension and it makes it more conceivable. So that was a case where being under was actually a giant advantage. It rarely is." Å

THE DEFIANT ONE

WRITTEN BY: Peter DeLuise DIRECTED BY: Peter DeLuise	GUEST CAST: Richard Ian Cox (Dr Gaul), Paul Magel (Dr Abrams), James Lafazanos (Wraith)

S cientists Dr Gaul and Dr Abrams accompany McKay and Sheppard on an expedition to the edges of the solar system to investigate a Lagrangian point satellite. Upon arrival, they discover that the massive weapons platform is completely inert, probably damaged when the Wraith finally besieged the Ancients in Atlantis. While in the vicinity, the puddle-jumper picks up a Wraith distress call coming from a nearby planet. Deciding to investigate, Sheppard lands, discovering a very old and apparently deserted Wraith ship. Inside are the bodies of many humans, and McKay surmises that this was a 'supply' ship originally bound for the front lines. It must have been shot down by the weapons platform and has been on the planet ever since. Sheppard is eager to explore, hoping that what they find could provide them with vital information about their enemy. However, McKay soon realizes that his original assumption that the Wraith pilot would be long dead is wrong. He's still alive, and is now determined to escape the planet with their ship. The Wraith attacks Dr Abrams and Dr Gaul, leaving Gaul barely alive to taunt Sheppard, who tries to prevent the Wraith from escaping with the puddle-jumper. Despite long years of hibernation, the Wraith is still stronger than the human, and Sheppard's attempts to kill the alien fail. Gaul, realizing that Sheppard needs McKay's help but that his friend won't leave him alone to die, makes the ultimate sacrifice and shoots himself. Even then, however, the pair are only saved when Ford and Teyla arrive on a rescue mission. The Wraith may have survived alone on a desert planet for centuries, but he proves no match for a direct missile strike.

DR GAUL: It's as large as a Goa'uld mothership. This could be the single largest weapons platform ever constructed.

"I got to try to envision what the Wraith were like 10,000 years ago," says writer and director Peter DeLuise, of his second trip into the *Stargate: Atlantis* universe. "I tried to create a more barbaric version of the Wraith, because they are quite stoic, more cool-headed than I think they would have been in the past. I left it a little ambiguous, but I tried to imply that the guy had been there for 10,000 years. He had been there since the original attack on Atlantis."

Opposite: Dr Abrams, Dr Gaul, McKay and Sheppard — intrepid explorers.

Unlike his first script for *Stargate: Atlantis*, 'Underground', with 'The Defiant One' DeLuise had the marked advantage of knowing the characters considerably better:

Above: James Lafazanos as a particularly feral Wraith.

"Because we had done a few shows and I knew where the characters were going, it was much, much easier to deal with. And because it was easier, because I knew what the characters would do, I could create more scenes that were poignant."

One aspect of this poignancy was in McKay's actions following the Wraith attack on his fellow scientist, Dr Gaul. "David Hewlett's character has evolved," says DeLuise. "If you remember him in *Stargate SG-1*, he had little or no heart. He was very aggressive, he was misogynistic towards Carter, and he was really quite full of himself and very selfish. In *Stargate: Atlantis*, he has continued to perpetuate the selfish thing, and the fact that he is quite full of himself and has a superiority complex. But what a lot of people didn't realize is that he does have a heart. Here, he had to help his friend as he died, had to comfort his friend in this terrible situation. This is when we see that he *does* have a heart. One of my directions to David was, 'You know that your friend is going to die, which means that you can be as caring and as sensitive as you want to be because he's going to die and no one will ever find out that you were a nice guy!' I think that struck a chord with David, because he was able to let his guard down. Whereas in a different situation to do that would be betraying his character, with this he was actually being true to it. His inner self came out and you see that this poor guy does have a heart and he isn't the bastard that everyone thinks he is!"

For guest actor James Lafazanos, playing the stranded Wraith was something of a new experience. Though he had played two other Wraith earlier in the series, this character was entirely different. "He's supposed to be ancient, even beyond the age of most Wraith," Lafazanos explains, "so I felt that he was kind of like an old pirate, because he was the commander of a ship that crash landed on this planet and he was the only remaining one because he ate all the cargo and his crew. That tells you something about him!"

'The Defiant One' also represented for Lafazanos the most specific directions he had received to date on how to portray the Wraith. "Peter DeLuise had a vision for sure, that this one Wraith was pretty much wild, a real brute that had no code of ethics at all, not even amongst Wraith. He was smart, but just animalistic. I remember on the days we were out there in the Richmond desert, he was really pushing me, more than any other episode with any other Wraith character, to really show the buck-wild animal that Wraith can be. And I think it came across."

The creation of this unnamed Wraith was assisted not only by Peter DeLuise's very specific vision for the character, but also by the location and weather. Mostly shot on the Richmond sand dunes at the height of summer, Lafazanos admits that at times, buried in the Wraith make-up and heavy costume, the experience was almost too much. "That was probably the most trying of the characters, that particular shoot," the actor reveals. "It was a really hot week, even for Vancouver, and it was a desert. I was under a lot of make-up, taking all the direction and trying to remember all the details of all the things you have to remember, amongst that heat."

McKAY: I swear there was nothing there when I scanned for life-signs.
SHEPPARD: They don't show up as life-signs when they're hibernating!

The production, having operated in similarly challenging conditions before, knew how to make the shoot as comfortable as possible, but it was still a struggle. "They were great — they set up a special little air conditioned tent for me, and I thank them for that," says Lafazanos. "Peter DeLuise really went out of his way to make sure I was okay, he's great that way. I had the make-up guys with little fans wherever I was and making sure I was well hydrated. But I think I had a personal trip in that desert! Being in the Wraith [make-up] for six days — my head was swimming a little bit," he laughs. "It reminds me of that desert sequence from *The Doors*, Oliver Stone's film. You kind of start tripping out a little bit. It was good, I had a great support system, but it was definitely challenging. There were times there that I really thought I was the Wraith, and that was trippy. You hear of actors that get lost in characters, and that was one of those moments. It was great for the character, but I enjoyed the break afterwards!" Å

HOT ZONE

WRITTEN BY: Martin Gero
DIRECTED BY: Mario Azzopardi

GUEST CAST: Paul McGillion (Dr Carson Beckett),
Craig Veroni (Dr Peter Grodin)

McKay, Zelenka and Ford lead a team of scientists to check the outskirts of Atlantis for storm damage. However, when they prepare to return to the center, two of the scientists are discovered as missing. They can be heard on the radio, distraught and apparently under attack. When located, one scientist is already dead and the other seems to be suffering from violent hallucinations, which precipitate her death in front of the whole team. Fearing a viral outbreak, McKay quarantines the search team and Beckett organizes a Hazmat team to examine them. Peterson, another scientist, panics. Meanwhile, Teyla and Sheppard are conducting a training session when Weir announces a city-wide quarantine, requesting that everyone stay where they are. Sheppard argues, but Weir orders him to stay put. McKay and the group of quarantine subjects search for the source of the disease, and find an Ancient laboratory that appears to have been used to research pathogens. While investigating, another member of McKay's team dies. Peterson, terrified, leaves the group and begins to head back to the center. If he reaches the city within, the whole of Atlantis could be infected. Sheppard, hearing this, overrides Weir's order so that he can stop Peterson himself, but Atlantis itself begins a lockdown when it senses a threat. McKay discovers that the sickness is a nanovirus designed to kill humans by rupturing an artery in the brain. McKay's first solution is a massive electromagnetic pulse from his lab, but this plan fails. Instead, Sheppard uses the puddle-jumper to detonate a nuclear explosion above Atlantis, which finally neutralizes the nanites.

BECKETT: Just try to stay calm.
FORD: Calm? You told me I have a million tiny robots running through my veins whose only purpose is to terrorize and kill me. You stay calm!

"I had just finished writing 'The Storm' and 'The Eye'," says Martin Gero of where the idea for 'Hot Zone' came from, "and Brad said, 'Look, you've just busted the bank for two episodes, go find me a way to save money! Have a show that we can shoot entirely on the sets that we own and it doesn't have a ton of effects.' So keeping that in mind, I thought about what would keep everybody in the same place — a disease of some sort. I originally wrote the outline without the visual apparitions, and Robert Cooper said, 'It's scary because people are dying, but we need to see what they

Opposite: Dr Beckett
fights a deadly foe.

MISSION ⊕ DEBRIEF

SGC

Atlantis' Self-Preservation

When the Ancients built their city, they incorporated several self-defense mechanisms, designed to protect the city and its inhabitants from attack — whether such an attack came from outside or from within the city itself. The first that the Atlantis expedition team encountered was the city's shield, which had held back the water of the planet's oceans for 10,000 years. Then, when the shield was too depleted in power to continue to keep the city safe, Atlantis herself sensed the danger and rose from the waves before the shield could collapse. Had Atlantis' Zero Point Modules not been dangerously depleted, this shield would have activated to protect the city from the superstorm that almost destroyed it in 'The Storm' and 'The Eye'. Atlantis also has a Stargate force shield, which activates when a traveler arrives from an unknown destination. Similar to the Earth's Stargate 'iris', the Atlantis gate force shield won't shut down unless the incoming traveler identifies themselves as safe. Finally, besides long-range scanners that can detect an incoming aerial threat, the city also has internal sensors capable of detecting and isolating a pathogen, and will isolate the carrier to protect other inhabitants.

are seeing. Because it's a nanovirus, it is a weapon of terror, so we should see that.'"

Though the finished episode is one of the best character-driven episodes of the season, to begin with the cast weren't too sure whether *Stargate: Atlantis'* first 'bottle show' (the term for a low-budget episode shot entirely in the studio) was going to be very 'hot' at all. "It's very difficult to make disease scary on film," points out David Hewlett. "It's been done a million times. I had heard there was a 'flu' episode coming up, and I thought, 'Oh no... it'll be a lot of "Don't breathe!" and masks and stuff.' But they got out of that brilliantly by including the visions. So you get a good horror story, and it adds so much more to the suspense. I was very happy with that one."

"When I read it, I thought, 'This is not going to be very good,'" agrees Joe Flanigan, "because the enemy is a nanovirus. How exciting is that? You can't see the enemy. You can't deal with the enemy. And once again," the actor continues, laughing, "as seems to be a pattern now, it turned out well and people loved it."

Another interesting aspect of 'Hot Zone' that would continue to develop as filming on the series progressed was the origin of the nanovirus itself, which introduced a whole new puzzle for the Atlantis fraternity. "The nanovirus was created by somebody other than the Wraith," Flanigan points out. "That's an extremely sophisticated thing and we thought, up until that point, that the Wraith were our arch-enemy."

'Hot Zone' was also something of a turning point in terms of the military-versus-civilian relationship between Dr Weir and Major Sheppard, which had hitherto been

very calm and cooperative. "Torri expressed some concern about it," Flanigan reveals, "because what she didn't want was there to be this habitual conflict between Sheppard and Weir, where Weir would say, 'Okay, go ahead and do it.' So we needed to give it some levels, and overriding her like that was one way of doing it. It sets itself up for conflict further down the road."

SHEPPARD: Should I pay attention to all these warnings? McKAY: Not today, no...

"We hadn't done it," explains Gero of why it was time for Weir and Sheppard to go head-to-head, "and we all kind of agreed that [here], they were both right, and that's a good time to do it. Weir was being overly cautious, I think, at the beginning, but then Sheppard got reckless towards the end. So it felt like a good time to make an issue of the fact that it's easy to get along when everything is going right, it's a lot more difficult to get along when everything's falling apart."

The episode also gave some new scope to the ever-developing character of Dr Beckett, to actor Paul McGillion's delight — notwithstanding the outfit he had to wear throughout the episode. "I think I lost about fifteen pounds!" exclaims the actor. "That was more of a 'heady' episode — it was a really interesting way to develop a villain like that. It's different — the Wraith are so visibly apparent, and this villain is sort of out of our hands. It was really interesting to play, and obviously when you're playing an entire episode in a Hazmat suit, you're sweating, you can't hear very well, and it's like you're acting in an echo chamber! So it's really challenging from an acting perspective." Å

SANCTUARY

WRITTEN BY: Alan Brennert
DIRECTED BY: James Head

GUEST CAST: Leonor Varela (Chaya Sar/Athar),
Paul McGillion (Dr Carson Beckett), Robert Thurston (Zarah),
Craig Veroni (Dr Peter Grodin)

The puddle-jumper is pursued by two Wraith Darts, but as it skims the atmosphere of a nearby planet, the Wraith ships are destroyed by an energy weapon from the surface. The team goes to investigate and discovers a non-industrialized civilization which apparently has no idea about either the Wraith or the weapon of which the team speak. Teyla feels that the planet could be a haven for refugees, since the small population uses hardly any of its resources. The leader of the village offers to take them to their high priestess, who can convene with their god, Athar, and ask if this would be appropriate. The team are taken to meet Chaya, a beautiful young woman who instantly forms a bond with Sheppard. However, she refuses their request, saying that Athar wants no one but her own people on the planet. Sheppard suggests that she return with them and visit Atlantis, to see that all humans are in effect 'Athar's people'. The woman agrees. Arriving in Atlantis, she undergoes a health check by Beckett, who reports to Weir that she is in perfect health — too perfect, in fact. McKay is also suspicious, and asks Weir to allow him to scan her covertly. Sheppard, unaware of their concerns, finds himself increasingly attracted to Chaya, but she still will not allow the planet to become a safe haven or admit that they have a weapon. When McKay scans her, he realizes the truth — her priestess lifestyle is simply a disguise for her true self. Chaya is an Ancient. Chaya confesses that she is in exile on the planet, punished centuries ago by her people for interfering in the affairs of man. Her punishment is to remain on the planet and defend that civilization, and no other. Lonely, she only came to Atlantis because of Sheppard, and is unable to even give them any information about her race. She has, however, activated a long-range scanner that they can use to detect approaching ships.

McKAY: Word of caution. The whole Captain Kirk routine is problematic, to say the least; let alone morally dubious.

'Sanctuary' was something of a departure from the all-out action of previous *Stargate: Atlantis* episodes, as the team finally came into contact with a living Ancient only to discover what Daniel and the *Stargate SG-1* team had found several years before — that just because the 'ascended' race is technologically and spiritually advanced doesn't mean that they necessarily always have the moral high ground. 'Sanctuary'

Opposite: The village's leader offers to take the team to see their high priestess.

SANCTUARY

Above: The Atlantis team
attempt to persuade Chaya
to help them.

was in fact a somewhat brutal reminder of the dark side of the Pegasus Galaxy, where one society can live in blissful ignorance while others around it suffer under the Wraith threat.

For once, too, Major Sheppard found himself distracted by thoughts of something other than the defense of the city as the soldier became more and more charmed by priestess Chaya. Sheppard falling in love, actor Joe Flanigan admits, wasn't an idea that really thrilled him. "I wasn't crazy about the idea of there being a romance," says Flanigan. "It wasn't the main storyline, but I thought it was a dangerous area to get into, because with the urgency of what's going on, sometimes romance can seem a little bit trivial under the generally life-threatening circumstances that we find in the scripts. So I was a little skeptical about it. It was bordering on new territory for the character, but I thought it turned out okay."

It was also a little frustrating for the rest of the Atlantis crew, particularly McKay and Weir. "It was definitely something that represents Weir's passion," says Torri Higginson. "This is exactly why she was chosen to be there, for her expertise in crossing cultural boundaries and being able to relate to different cultures and her understanding of the language," the actress laughs, "but they got all googly-eyed and nobody else could reach her!"

One of the most striking aspects of the episode were the spectacular sets developed by Bridget McGuire and her crew. "'Sanctuary' actually had two fairly nice sets," says the production designer. "We did the village out at the lake, and we were kind of scavengers there," she says with a laugh. "There were some frames of the buildings out there that we used as our basis. I think it was a camp or something like that, and we went out there and stripped off all the metal and then used thatch and bamboo and made it into a nice little town."

The second set developed for the episode had actually already appeared in the *Stargate SG-1* universe: "The temple for 'Sanctuary' was a re-use from a *Stargate SG-1* set for the episode 'It's Good to be King'. Originally it was a medieval town thing, and we stripped all of that out and piled greens into it to change it around that way. I used that set for four episodes last season — 'It's Good to be King', 'Sanctuary', 'The Brotherhood' and then 'Moebius'. By the end of it we had gone from it being an exterior medieval street to an interior dungeon! Then we also used it for a green set as well — so I used it five times in total. For the last time that we used it, I needed to build a green set which was forest and trees," McGuire explains. "Quite often if they need a forest environment for one scene, it's not worth us going out on location to do it. We need a whole day's shooting for us to go out to a forest. So in that case I'll have the greens department make a bit of forest somewhere on set. And in this case the forest was in that set because I had run out of studio space! It was the only place free!"

CHAYA: We will know each other as well as anyone ever can.

SHEPPARD: Okay... if I get the car back by midnight though.

'Sanctuary' also benefited from the expert costume designs of Christina McQuarrie, who had a chance to abandon the uniforms and earth-tones that had dominated *Stargate: Atlantis* costumes in the first year and go for something completely different. "That came from a script direction," say the costume designer of the episode's South Pacific islander feel. "So the designs came from a certain amount of research, and also from trying to tweak reality. You look at the historical references and then just try and tweak it so that it doesn't look like you're going directly to Fiji or Polynesia." Å

BEFORE I SLEEP

WRITTEN BY: Carl Binder
DIRECTED BY: Andy Mikita

GUEST CAST: Gildart Jackson (Janus), Paul McGillion (Dr Beckett), David Nykl (Dr Zelenka), Craig Veroni (Dr Grodin)

Sheppard's team discovers a cryogenically frozen woman left behind when the Atlanteans fled the city. When the old woman wakes, she makes a stunning claim — she is actually Elizabeth Weir. Beckett verifies this with a DNA match, and Dr Weir finds herself faced with a centuries-old version of herself. 'Old Weir' tells her story — when the Atlantis expedition first came through the Stargate, there was no contingent for the city's shield failing. The city did not rise from the ocean and the resulting flood killed everyone but Weir, Sheppard and Zelenka, who made it to a puddle-jumper which was shot down with Weir the only survivor. Rescued from the wreckage by the inhabitants of Atlantis, Weir discovered that the puddle-jumper they used was in fact a timeship that had taken her back to Atlantis' last stand against the Wraith. The Ancients refused to allow Weir to return to her time — so instead, the timeship's creator worked out a system whereby she could go into stasis, waking three times over 10,000 years, rotating the power in the ZPMs to keep Atlantis going on minimal power. That way, the 'next' time the Earth team arrived, the city would rise from the deep instead of letting its shield collapse. It clearly worked, and the Atlantis team's survival is evidence of just that. Though she does not survive long once out of stasis, 'Old Weir' does have time to explain the note she carries with her — a list of gate addresses with planets known to have working ZPMs.

OLD WEIR: Look at you. I didn't think I'd see any of you again. I missed you all so terribly. Even you, Rodney.

"I was fascinated by Weir from the first time I read the pilot," says writer Carl Binder. "There's a moment where someone says something to the effect of, 'You're in charge, you just have to believe it. You just have to have faith in yourself.' I really loved the idea of this woman who's putting up this front but who has these insecurities that she doesn't want to show anyone. Then I coupled that with the idea that Atlantis is a very big place and they are continuing to explore the city — one of the things they discover is a lab in which there is an 'Ancient' in a stasis chamber, who turns out to be Weir. What a great opportunity for her to see herself as a 10,000 year-old person! She's had 10,000 years to think about herself. That gives the sort of insight that only you can provide for yourself. That fascinated me."

Binder wrote 'Before I Sleep' as a freelancer. "I pitched to Brad Wright and Robert [C. Cooper] and then sat in the room with the whole gang and broke the

Opposite: Weir prepares to go to 'sleep'.

BEFORE I SLEEP

story," he recalls. "What I pitched was the discovery of the 'Ancient' woman who turns out to be Weir. From there, we worked it all out together and then I went off and wrote the script.

The script changed very little on its way to the screen, although the writer reports that one favorite moment didn't make it to the final cut. "It was a scene where Weir takes 'Old Weir' out in her wheelchair and shows her around Atlantis," Binder explains. "As it is in the episode right now, they then cut to inside the conference room, where they continue to talk. But [originally] I had 'Young Weir' push 'Old Weir' out onto the balcony overlooking the ocean. 'Old Weir' takes in the fresh air and says, 'I haven't smelled fresh air in over 10,000 years.' It's about that longing of hers to be out in the open — so that at the end, when 'Young Weir' releases her ashes into the air, it had a bit more resonance. I kind of wish that had made it in, but those things happen. Andy [Mikita] said it was just because of time."

For director Andy Mikita, 'Before I Sleep' marked his first introduction to directing a full episode of *Stargate: Atlantis*. 'Before I Sleep' was a significant episode due to the extensive make-up that Torri Higginson had to undergo as 'Old Weir', and Mikita admits that the make-up was a concern from the outset. "I was worried about making sure that Torri was comfortable and able to feel good about being in the make-up, because a lot of people who have never done it before can have a very rough first experience. It was tough, because although we have one of the best special effects make-up crews in North America, and they were very efficient with the application, Torri still had to be in the make-up trailer at 3.30am for a 7.30am call. It was a very long working day."

Sheppard: ...not to mention a really nice DeLorean.
McKAY: Don't even get me started on that movie!

To help lessen Higginson's hours, Mikita and the crew adjusted the shooting schedule. "Once she was in the make-up for the first time, I decided that, 'I'm not going to be able to subject this poor girl to day after day of going under prosthetics at 3am in the morning!' So Torri and I spoke to the other actors and the crew and we decided that just for the sake of her comfort, we would go through the entire script and block shoot everything with her in the make-up. So when we shot the scenes with her as 'Old Weir' in the infirmary, we shot everything relating to her in the bed in one day. That was not the original plan, but in hindsight, it was definitely the right thing to do."

Something else that altered during filming was the method used to film Higginson speaking to herself as both ages. "We had hired two additional actresses, one to be in old-age make-up similar to Torri and another who was basically a photo-double for Torri when in her regular 'Young Weir' look. We ended up using those two a lot more than we had initially anticipated."

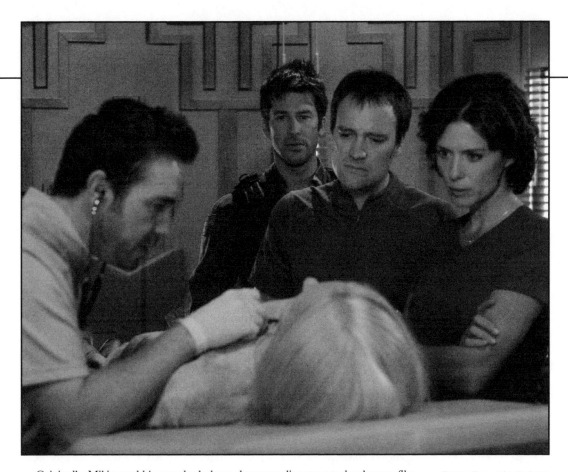

Above: Weir gets to know
herself a little better.

Originally, Mikita and his crew had planned to use split-screen technology to film the scenes in which the 'Young' and 'Old Weir' interact. "The split-screens that we had attempted to use didn't really work out too well," the director explains. "So we just ended up using the other actor and photo-double, which worked really well because they knew their lines so Torri could work with them. Also, I had a video surveillance camera on Torri at all times when she was in make-up. Then when we took off the make-up and brought her back to her regular self, we played back the video on a monitor beside the bed, so that Torri was in effect both on playback screen and monitor at the same time. So, from the audience's perspective, they could see both looks. That's a little device that ended up working pretty well, I think."

"By and large, I was pleased," says Mikita of the finished episode. "One of the challenges was intercutting existing footage from the pilot, and in fact, we restaged a scene that was to be done as an absolute duplicate of a shot in the pilot, but then at a particular point the 'Before I Sleep' story takes a turn and the performances change and the audience realizes, 'Oh, wait — this is not from the pilot, this is different.' I was really pleased with how that worked. The one thing as directors we all strive for is to do justice to the script. I hope we did." Å

THE BROTHERHOOD

WRITTEN BY: Martin Gero
DIRECTED BY: Martin Wood

GUEST CAST: Jana Mitsoula (Allina), Robert Davi (Commander Acastus Kolya), Laura Mennel (Sanir), David Nykl (Dr Zelenka), Paul McGillion (Dr Beckett)

Using the list of known Zero Point Modules in the Pegasus Galaxy given to them by 'Old Weir', Sheppard, McKay, Ford and Teyla visit a planet called Dagan. A historical researcher named Allina reveals that what they call the 'Potentia' was a religious relic amongst their people, protected by a religious order called the Quindozum. The myth goes that an Ancient arrived through the gate and instructed the Dagans to keep the Potentia hidden, which the Brotherhood did only too well — now, centuries later, the knowledge of where the relic is hidden is lost. McKay works with Allina to locate the Potentia, though there are elements among the Dagans who do not believe they should help the outsiders find their most holy religious treasure. Meanwhile, the Genii have tracked Sheppard and his team and a now-recovered Kolya decides to intercept the team on Dagan. Using the dissention amongst the Dagans, the Genii arrive on the planet and capture the team, forcing McKay and Allina to find the ZPM and hand it over. In Atlantis, Zelenka discovers that the city has deep space sensors — and there's a Wraith Dart headed straight for the city. Weir mobilizes the puddle-jumpers but the enemy ship destroys one before scanning the city and self destructing. On Dagan, Sheppard and Ford manage to take back the ZPM, but Allina herself reclaims it. Having discovered that the visitors are not originally from Atlantis, she has decided to hide the Potentia again to prevent it being used, and nothing McKay or Sheppard says can persuade her. Atlantis still has no new power source. Worse, Atlantis' deep space sensors have discovered that three hive ships are headed for Atlantis, and will be over the planet within two weeks.

KOLYA: The smart thing to do would be to kill me now.
SHEPPARD: You're right. I'm going to want points for this in the future. But if you ever do this again, I _will_ kill you.

"'The Brotherhood' is my favorite episode of the year that I wrote," reveals Martin Gero. "It was possibly the hardest one to write, but good because it was fun."

The difficulty, the writer reveals, came in the task he set himself when he first pitched the idea to the rest of *Stargate: Atlantis'* producers. "It's easy to say 'We'll do kind of an *Indiana Jones*-type episode where McKay unlocks the secret of this hidden society,'" says Gero with a dry laugh. "Everyone says 'great!' But then you have to go think of the secrets of the hidden society, and write it in such a way so you

Opposite: Teyla finds a clue.

THE BROTHERHOOD

Above: So close, and yet so far — Allina, McKay and Sheppard struggle with the puzzle of the fifteen.

can figure it out, but it can't be so obvious that the audience says, 'Well, these people were idiots for not having figured that out before.'"

To complete the route of McKay and co's quest, Gero decided that a different approach was needed. "I came up with the final puzzle, which was the magic square with the numbers one to nine that can be placed in a three by three grid to add up to fifteen in every direction. I came up with that and then worked backwards, and built the whole thing about the Brotherhood of the fifteen and the nine stone carriers. That was really the only way that I could attack it."

The writer also gives full praise to the *Stargate: Atlantis* art department, who were given the task of visualizing Gero's puzzle. "Again, it was easy for me to write something like, 'You look at the stones and it looks like a map but it's really gate addresses and you can't really tell until they're all together,'" he says. "It's another thing to then give that to the art department and have them actually make it! So it was really just exciting from one stage to the next. The art department did such a great job with just little tiny details that probably only [director] Martin Wood and myself will ever see."

For Martin Wood, who had previously directed *Stargate: Atlantis*' stunning two-part episodes 'Rising' and 'The Storm'/'The Eye', directing 'The Brotherhood' was not only fun, but also a welcome change of pace. "When Brad Wright and Martin Gero called me in and said this was going to be the next one, I thought, 'This is neat!' It was a lot of fun making 'The Brotherhood', because we were shooting out in the hot weather. It was opportunistic too, because I had just finished 'The Storm' and 'The Eye' and had this other big two-parter coming up ['The Siege'] and I had just started preparing for that. I thought okay, 'The Brotherhood' is a perfect stand-alone episode that just allows me to direct and not spend a lot of time concentrating on logistics. It was nice to settle down and do a single episode."

McKAY: There may very well be hundreds of Zero Point Modules hidden in this galaxy, but the only one we are remotely sure of is here. If you ever want to go home, if you ever want to protect Atlantis from the Wraith, we need to find this.

"That's about as romantic as McKay gets — a good dig in a field somewhere!" David Hewlett says with a laugh, revealing that while shooting in the Vancouver sun might have been good for the director, for him it was a different matter entirely. "It was another really difficult one to film, quite honestly. Those location ones are killers. Some people enjoy them, but I'm not terribly outdoorsy I'm afraid! But it was like shooting *Indiana Jones*! I think, to me, that's very indicative of the old *Stargate SG-1* kind of stuff, where they're out there solving puzzles and trying to find things before someone else does. It was all nicely interwoven, and there was some really very funny stuff."

In fact, one of the actor's favorite scenes of the episode — a sentiment shared by writer Martin Gero — didn't make it into the final cut. "It does have my favorite cut scene," says Gero. "There was a scene at the beginning where they are making fun of Ford. It starts with Sheppard and Teyla and Ford going through these books that they don't understand, and so it's kind of just devolved into small chat about their first kiss. It was just a fun little scene. It was a great character scene but we were a little long on that episode — we were maybe having a little too much fun! At the end of the day when you're looking for things to cut, it wasn't important to the story so that was the first thing to go." Å

LETTERS FROM PEGASUS

WRITTEN BY: Carl Binder
DIRECTED BY: Mario Azzopardi

GUEST CAST: Amanda Tapping (Major Samantha Carter), Gary Jones (Sergeant Walter Harriman), David Nykl (Dr Zelenka), Paul McGillion (Dr Carson Beckett), Ben Cotton (Dr Kavanagh), Terence Kelly (Orin)

As the team discusses solutions to the problem of the approaching Wraith hive ships, McKay announces that he may be able to send a brief message to Earth. Though it could risk overloading the city's all-important Naquada generators, the scientist thinks he can open a wormhole to the SGC for 1.3 seconds, and use his tailored compression ratios to send all of their mission reports, information they've learnt about the Wraith, and much more besides. Weir tells McKay to go ahead, aware that Earth is unlikely to be able to send help or they would have already done so. However, she feels it is important that they warn Earth about the Wraith threat, if nothing else. As Atlantis begins to gather as much information to send to Earth as they can, Weir appoints Ford to record personal messages from the expedition members. Meanwhile, Zelenka has used the city's deep space sensors to plot where the Wraith hive ships will stop to make feeding raids. Sheppard and Teyla plan to intercept one such raid and observe with the aim of gathering useful intelligence. However, Teyla wants to do much more, and tries to persuade the major to save a family friend from the Wraith. At first reluctant, when they become stuck on the planet and it becomes clear they will have to wait out the attack, he agrees to help. Observing the raid, both Teyla and Sheppard realize the scale of the coming assault on Atlantis — it's going to be bad. Very, very bad.

WEIR: We have to warn Earth.
SHEPPARD: Even if it's the last thing we do?
WEIR: Especially if it's the last thing we do.

As the first year of *Stargate: Atlantis* sped towards its conclusion, the producers needed to implement several important movements in the season's arc, one of which being Earth's all-important receipt of Atlantis' frantic transmission. It was also about time for a standard television money-saving device — the clip show episode, usually designed to claw back some all-important budget in readiness for the season finale. Under Brad Wright and Robert Cooper's supervision, *Stargate SG-1*'s 'clip shows' had always been written around an ingenious plot, and with 'Letters From Pegasus', *Stargate: Atlantis* followed that trend — even if at first, no one could quite decide whether the episode was actually a clip show or not.

"When I finished 'Before I Sleep', Brad asked me if I would be interested in doing another one," explains writer Carl Binder. "He already had the story — 'Letters From

Opposite: Teyla tries to help a friend.

Pegasus'. At first he said, 'Well, it's going to be a clip show.' Then he said, 'Well it might not be a clip show.' He eventually saw it as not quite a clip show, but a show in which the clips are very quick. They are more glimpses than anything. So it was never designed as a full-on clip show, but it always was designed to have some clips in it. In some ways it was more difficult than 'Before I Sleep', because I didn't work out the story with everyone in the room with everyone else for that one. I was working a little more in the dark."

As a result, the finished script did go through several changes as executive producer Brad Wright hammered it into shape, showing what a collaborative affair a story is for the *Stargate: Atlantis* team. "A lot of what I put in is still there, but he ended up doing a lot more reworking on that one," explains the writer. "The Japanese assistant, that was all pretty much mine, and McKay's letters. Weir's letters home to the families of the people that died, Brad added all that to it, and the Sheppard and Teyla story on the other planet."

"I really enjoyed that one," says Torri Higginson. "I thought that was a sweet one. I remember reading it and thinking, 'Gosh, this is already a big show,' and that was a nice feeling. I was also really glad that Weir took it on herself to contact all the families — I thought that was a very Weir thing to do."

'Letters From Pegasus' also gave Higginson a chance to write her own lines for Weir for a scene which the actress felt particularly strongly about. "The video message to Simon changed," the actress explains, "because originally in the first script she was saying, 'I love you honey, I love you.' I went to the producers and said, 'That doesn't seem like her. She doesn't know if she's going to survive, or when she'll be back, and it seems like a very selfish thing to say, "I have the right to ask you to wait for me."' And Brad Wright was great, he just said, 'Say whatever you want.' So that was nice."

FORD: Well, who do you wish was here?
BECKETT: Nobody! I wish I wasn't bloody here!

Rainbow Sun Francks also reports that he found 'Letters From Pegasus' one of the most rewarding for the character of Aiden Ford. "We switch from 'Military Ford' to total 'Civilian Ford', and that's really nice that you get to see just Aiden. He gets to talk to everyone just as a person — except for Kavanagh, who really pisses him off," laughs Francks. "That's one of my favorite episodes of the season for that very reason. I was in control of a lot of scenes and there was some great stuff happening. I got to talk more loosely, it's not just 'Yes sir. No sir' stuff. That was really fun for me to do. And it was just funny, because that was one of the episodes that when we saw it on paper the whole cast reading it was thinking, 'Oh, I don't know about this — a clip show?' And then we saw it, and we were like, 'Wow, that was a great episode.' It summed the season up really nicely and it wasn't at all contrived."

"Carl Binder did such a great job," agrees Paul McGillion. "He does have that sense of compassion, and there is some humor in there as well. I really loved 'Letters From Pegasus' as a clip show — sometimes those can be hit or miss, but I thought it was great, and it really established how much they had gone through in that year. I thought everybody had their moments and Rainbow did a great job, and the scenes between Joe and Rachel in the puddle-jumper were just great. There is some real dramatic tension there which juxtapositioned the comedy, and I thought it was a really nice synopsis episode." Å

Above: Sheppard sees the power of the Wraith at first hand.

THE GIFT

WRITTEN BY: Robert C. Cooper and Martin Gero
DIRECTED BY: Peter DeLuise

GUEST CAST: Paul McGillion (Dr Beckett), David Nykl (Dr Zelenka), Ben Cotton (Dr Kavanagh), Claire Rankin (Dr Heightmeyer)

Teyla begins to suffer from severe nightmares about the Wraith. With just a week before the Wraith armada arrives, Atlantis is on full alert and trying to find ways to survive, which includes McKay trying to find a way of activating the Ancient defense control chair and to locate a safe Alpha site. After talking to psychologist Kate Heightmeyer, Teyla decides that she needs to investigate her ability to sense the Wraith. She visits the mainland, where an Athosian elder tells her of a group of humans returned by the Wraith. These people were disturbed, hearing voices and becoming violent. The villagers turned on them, killing most and driving the rest away. One of the survivors was an ancestor of Teyla's. Though the village is now in ruins, Sheppard's team visits and discovers a hidden Wraith laboratory. They bring back a data recorder which Weir begins to translate, discovering that the Wraith language is a derivative of Ancient. She also discovers that the Wraith who was conducting the experiment was doing so against the wishes of the hive — more importantly, Teyla has Wraith DNA, which is what enables her to sense the Wraith. The experiments inadvertently linked the test subjects to the Wraith hive mind. Teyla's abilities are a residual effect of this — and with effort, she may be able to connect to them deliberately, giving Atlantis all the intelligence they need. Using hypnotherapy this does seem to be the case, but through Teyla the Wraith can also access Atlantis. Almost immediately the Alpha site is attacked. Teyla penetrates the Wraith ship again, seeing their attack route. She also discovers the Wraith want more than to wipe Atlantis out — they need more food. They need Earth.

Teyla: Everyone on this base is probably afraid. I do not know why I am bothering you.
Heightmeyer: Have you always been able to sense the Wraith?

"The great thing about this was it finally dealt with Teyla," says director Peter DeLuise. "And that was a long time coming, because all we knew about her was that she had some special powers that were kind of ambiguous. We didn't know what they were. She could kind of sense the Wraith, but why, we didn't know, and she could fight real good, which was one of the reasons for her being one of the leaders of her community."

Having spent a year working alongside Rachel Luttrell in the guise of Teyla, DeLuise was glad to have an opportunity to help the actress explore her character

Opposite: Dr Heightmeyer helps Teyla to explore her new abilities.

further. "Rachel is a wonderful actress, but she didn't have a whole lot to do," he explains. "She would carry a gun and kick people's asses, and the fact that she wasn't raising her eyebrow and saying 'Indeed' a lot was the only thing that separated her from Teal'c! It can actually be a very tedious thing to be an alien on the show, because you don't always have a lot to do. And Rachel is so professional and so wonderful — she never complains and she always knows her lines. It finally came time for us to learn a little bit more about her character, and Robert Cooper wrote a wonderful episode about Teyla's background. It was very cool working with Rachel. She's such a great actress and she really got to show that off."

For the actress herself, the episode represented an opportunity for her to explore more about her enigmatic alter-ego, who had hitherto only shown her strongest side to the viewer. "It helped broaden the audience's understanding of Teyla," says Luttrell. "'The Gift' dove into why she had these physical capabilities and we got to see some of her people and her confidant among her people, this wonderful wise old woman."

The episode also saw Teyla learning something new about the human experience, when she is introduced to Dr Heightmeyer by Major Sheppard. Luttrell explains that the scenes in which Teyla underwent psychoanalysis at the hands of a doctor from Earth were some of the most difficult to film of the episode: "It's so difficult for Teyla to open up and show her frailty. She is slowly developing something similar to that with some of the other characters, but to open up to this complete stranger — that was a difficult thing for me to gauge. How much would Teyla want to reveal, and how comfortable would she be with emotions? And even though I was addressing incredibly personal aspects of who she was, I didn't want to [over play it]. Teyla wouldn't break down

MISSION Ⓐ DEBRIEF

SGC

Wraith Experiments

The Wraith, besides being a fearsome enemy, have in the past experimented with ways of making their 'herd' of humans a more efficient food source. When these experiments had side effects undesirable to the Wraith, their scientists were ordered to halt immediately. At least one Wraith scientist did not, however — his experiments resulted in certain people of the Athosian race in particular being left with the ability to sense the Wraith. For some, the experiments and their side effects went even further. Teyla Emmagan discovered that she herself had the ability to probe so deeply into a Wraith's mind that she could actually take over its consciousness, allowing her 'inside' a Wraith hive ship. This works both ways, however, since the Wraith, once connected to Teyla's mind, can also explore her surroundings, posing a distinct security threat.

Above: Getting to the bottom of Teyla's connection to the Wraith proves painful for the whole team.

and cry, for instance. She would always show some kind of strength, whereas you or I, in the same situation, would maybe be a little more frail. That whole situation for her was completely new and bizarre. And the only reason she found herself there was because she felt she had no other choice."

Through the information Teyla provides during the course of the episode, the Atlanteans also discover the imminence of the coming Wraith attack — and viewers have a chance to see right inside a fully operational hive ship. "When she psychically projects herself into the Wraith ship, we are able to see great footage of the Wraith carrying on doing their thing," says director DeLuise. "That's been a bit of a mystery in the past. The episode also helps us understand a little more about the Wraith — that they don't just eat people all day long!"

Teyla: What was he doing?
Beckett: I think he was trying to make their food source more compatible with their species.

The episode also saw another first for the character of Teyla, as she loses a training bout to Major Sheppard. "Well, you know what," says Luttrell with a laugh, "they say that it takes a really good singer to sing badly — not to say that I'm a fantastic fighter, because God knows I'm still learning a hell of a lot, but I think it was similar! It was hard because I'm used to Teyla being really strong and having the upper hand, but in a way I enjoyed that just as much as I did some of her stronger scenes, because it was great to show that weaker side of her. But in the same way that she was quite physically weak, she was still mentally strong, in that she wanted to continue the fight. Even though she was getting beaten, she kept getting back on her feet and saying, 'Let's go, let's do it again,' until finally Sheppard was unwilling to push it." Å

THE SIEGE (I)

WRITTEN BY: Martin Gero
DIRECTED BY: Martin Wood

GUEST CAST: Paul McGillion (Dr Beckett), David Nykl (Dr Zelenka), Craig Veroni (Dr Grodin), Christopher Heyerdahl (Halling)

With time running out before the Wraith armada arrives, McKay, Grodin and Miller travel to the Ancient defense satellite in the hope that they can repair it in time for when the Wraith ships pass by in forty-nine hours. If they can use it to destroy the ships before they even reach Atlantis, everyone will be saved. Meanwhile, Sheppard continues searching for another Alpha site and Zelenka tries to find a way of destroying Atlantis so the Stargate — and the Wraith's route to Earth's galaxy — is blocked. Teyla returns to active duty much to Bates' disgust, since he is convinced that her link to the Wraith is giving away valuable information about their movements. When Bates is later discovered knocked out, Teyla is the obvious suspect — until Beckett finds Wraith DNA in his wounds. Locating the infiltrator, Sheppard and Ford take the Wraith, 'Bob', prisoner. Reaching the satellite, Grodin and McKay manage to fix the firing mechanism, but then discover that they can't retrieve Grodin from inside the satellite. With time running out, McKay and Miller use the puddle-jumper's cloak to hide from the approaching fleet. Grodin takes one of the hive ships out manually before the satellite breaks down again — and he's a sitting duck as the other two ships destroy the weapons platform. Distraught, McKay and Miller can do nothing but return to Atlantis, the city's only line of defense now gone. Sheppard, desperate for information, cannot get 'Bob' to talk and so shoots him dead. Weir, with all other avenues blocked, orders the evacuation of Atlantis.

TEYLA: Perhaps you are not aware, sergeant, but being accused of serving the Wraith is the greatest insult among my people.
BATES: Oh, I'm _aware_.

For director Martin Wood, 'The Siege' marked a stunning culmination of the first year of hard work on _Stargate: Atlantis_. "'The Siege' is amazing," he says enthusiastically. "When we did the pilot, there was a lot of explanation that had to happen, so pilots tend to be a little bit slow because you have to get everything started. Then we did 'The Storm' and 'The Eye', and they really started to move along a lot faster, because things were established and we could spend a little more on visual effects. Then we needed something to end with a bang, and 'The Siege' came along. It's huge. Of the three two-parters I did for the first year, 'The Siege' was the biggest."

Opposite: 'Bob' thinks
he has the upper hand...

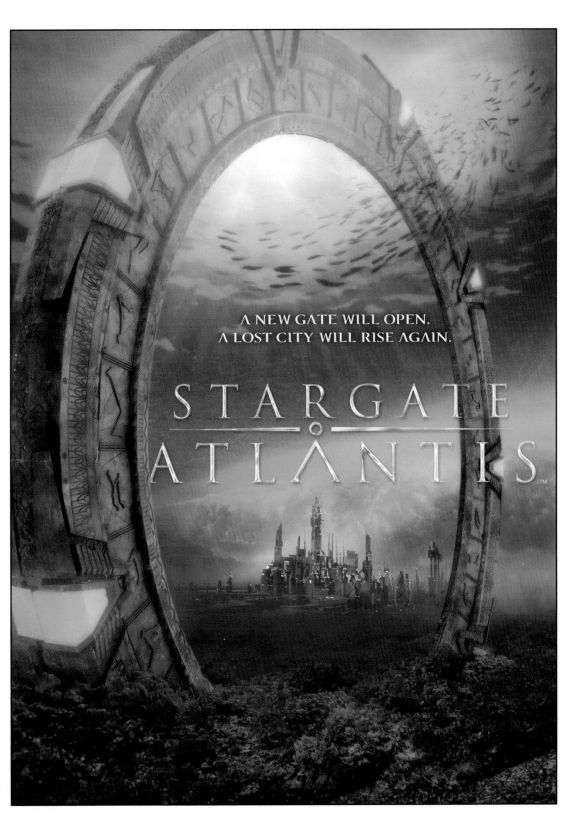

stage 1 - closed
(Unarmed)

step 2 - grenade is pulled open and ....step 3 - twisted 90 degrees in opposite directions,
& pushed back together

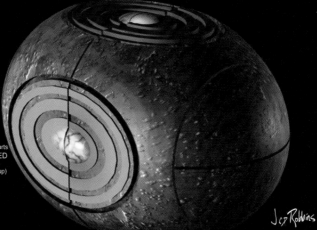

armed grenade

holding down any of the buttons starts
a delay timer - WHEN RELEASED
(visually the buttons should glow as
if on a dimmer being slowly turned up)

J c,D Robbins

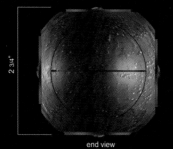

2 3/4"

end view

EPISODE	Defiant One		EPISODE # 013
STUDIO/LOCATION	Model Shop / Props		DATE June 16/04	SCALE as noted
DRAWING TITLE	Wraith Grenade		

STARGATE ATLANTIS

| BW | RC | MG | RDA | NJS | AM | PD | MW | PW | AP | BM | Const-3 | Paint-2 | Set Dec-3 | Model Shop | Props | Loc | Greens | SPFX | VFX | Grips | Light | Costumes | Make-up | Boyd | AD | Director | FLE | GH |

1-1 100% scale

4 1/4"

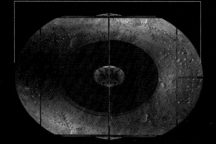

side (closed)

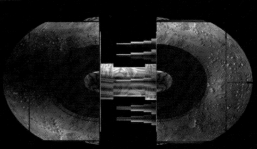

side (open)

The episode also saw a confrontation that the audience knew was going to come sooner or later, as Teyla took on Sergeant Bates in a head-to-head bout that saw the diminutive alien woman definitely come out on top! "We had a lot of fun coming up with just how that punch was going to happen," recalls the actress with a laugh. "Dean Marshall, who plays Bates, is just so much fun to work with. We had a blast with that particular section of the script! That was a lot of fun, swinging that punch. Obviously the two of us are going to be butting heads again in future episodes!"

The first part of 'The Siege' also saw the final approach of the Wraith armada and, as they neared the city, an indication of the sort of loss those in the city of Atlantis could expect, as a face that had been with the expedition since it's first days was killed in the line of duty. For Martin Wood, finding the right way to film the death of Craig Veroni's recurring character Peter Grodin was of paramount importance as an indication of what was yet to come in the series.

"There are two scenes that really affected me," says the director. "One was where I had Craig alone in the satellite. He knew it was going to be the last time we saw him, and I knew it was going to be the last time we saw him. He came up to me and said, 'What would you like me to do?' He was very emotional at that point, because he wanted to do it right and so did I, but he wanted it to be a bit of a send off for him." Wood realized, however, that for the scene to have the maximum impact, Grodin's sacrifice would have to be understated.

MISSION ⊕ DEBRIEF

SGC

Lagrangian Point Satellites

Celestial mechanics dictate that if there are two planets in orbit around a central object (for example a sun), there will be five points, known as Lagrangian points, outside the orbits of those two bodies where an object can be placed and will maintain their position without drifting into the orbit of their neighbors. The Ancients, knowing this, developed huge defense satellites to help keep Atlantis safe from the Wraith. Though most of them were destroyed centuries ago, the new Atlanteans discovered that one of them was still intact, though damaged (see 'The Defiant One'). These vast defense satellites are equipped with an arsenal big enough to destroy a Wraith fleet when working at optimum efficiency. Since the satellite takes less than two minutes to fully power up, it is possible to manually operate the satellite's firepower, making sure that the satellite remains dormant until the target is within range. Unfortunately, having temporarily repaired the remaining satellite to try and stop the approaching Wraith armada, it was destroyed when it malfunctioned again, killing Dr Peter Grodin along with the city's only chance of halting the enemy's advance.

"I thought, there's no way to linger on this, because then we're going to give it away. There had to be this lead up of 'Who is it going to be?' So we draw straws — that to me was an important point. There's this point where McKay has to go outside — so is it going to be McKay? McKay goes outside, and suddenly it's the not being able to get back in that becomes the problem, not the jeopardy of being out there. And I loved that, I thought that was brilliantly written, where the person that we thought was the safest because he's still inside the satellite is now the one that's in trouble. That scene where the camera lifts up and the sparks are falling past us and Craig is just looking up, saying goodbye — that shot, for me, was one of my favorite parts of 'The Siege' part one. The next thing that was really important was shooting David Hewlett's reaction. It was very simple, just a drifting camera across the front, and I let the actors do it on their own."

GRODIN: You can fix anything.
McKAY: Who told you that?
GRODIN: You did, on several occasions.

The death of Grodin and the destruction of the satellite marked a turning point in the episode, which from that point on saw events spiraling to chaos for the Atlantis team. One particularly powerful scene saw John Sheppard shoot dead the Wraith prisoner they had captured.

"That was pretty intense," agrees James Lafazanos, who did his own stunts for the scene. "There was almost a personal thing going on between them. They really don't know each other, but there was this energy that says that they do, almost. Like these two souls have been fighting it out for lifetimes, so it made for some really interesting energy between the two, I think. Especially since it got Sheppard's character to the point where he is filling him full of bullets, and in such a way that it was uncharacteristic of Sheppard. 'Bob' really brought something out in Sheppard that day that Sheppard didn't even know about himself." Å

THE SIEGE (II)

WRITTEN BY: Joseph Mallozzi / Paul Mullie

DIRECTED BY: Martin Wood

GUEST CAST: David Nykl (Dr Zelenka), Paul McGillion (Dr Carson Beckett), Christopher Britton (Prenum), Clayton Landey (Colonel Dillon Everett)

Weir orders Zelenka to implement their self-destruct plan, and the new Atlanteans prepare to leave the city for good, taking the Stargate control chip in the hope that they can some day return to Earth. However, as they dial out, an incoming wormhole blocks their way. The IDC is Earth's — the SGC have sent help to defend Atlantis in the form of Colonel Dylan Everett, who relieves Weir of her command. They have a ZPM, which will be brought to Pegasus by Earth's new battle cruiser, the Daedalus, which will reach Atlantis in four days. All they have to do is defend the city until then. Everett's top weapons are a batch of Naquada-enhanced nuclear warheads. The plan is to use the cloaked jumpers to place them as mines, but Everett ignores Sheppard's advice to keep two bombs in reserve. Sheppard is ordered to operate the Ancient chair, using the Naquada generator brought by the relief troops, but when they activate it McKay realizes that the chair has very few drones left — worse, Everett's decision to use all the warheads as mines backfires when the Wraith fire dozens of meteors towards them, detonating the bombs and wiping out Atlantis' only line of defense. After surviving the first wave of attacking Darts, the chair is useless and they are out of warheads. Weir manages to convince the Genii to use the attack to test their first nuclear bomb, which they can load onto a remote-controlled puddle-jumper to launch down the hive ship's throat. However, the remote system goes into meltdown, leaving Sheppard with no other option but to pilot the loaded puddle-jumper in a desperate suicide mission.

Everett: You have three Wraith hive ships bearing down on your position and precious little to defend yourselves with. That about sum it up?

"I was a little nervous about having anybody from Earth come in and contact us," admits Joe Flanigan, "because it can be an easy mechanism to fall back on. Before, we had to be ingenious and had to come up with things right on the spot. But then we wouldn't have had the epic battle that took place and we probably wouldn't have survived. So I liked that. But I was nervous about the contact with Earth."

In fact, 'The Siege' part two was worrying for the cast simply from the standpoint of wondering whether they all had jobs to return to for the second season! The frenetic action and new faces all pointed to a shake up for *Stargate: Atlantis*, as is very

Opposite: Help arrives from the SGC, but it may not be enough.

Above: Sheppard, Weir and McKay welcome some unexpected assistance.

common at the climax of a show's first year. "I think everybody, when we read that script, all went, 'Oh God, it's the end of the season and they're bringing in new characters — are we all fired?'" Torri Higginson laughs. Weir was one of the worst affected, with Everett's arrival leading to an unceremonious relief of command: "One panics a bit! But I thought it was going to be interesting to see Weir shaken up. Vulnerability is always nice to play and it was nice because we were all put in that position. Sheppard and Weir were both feeling that — it made us feel that we were a family, us against them."

This emotional theme is threaded throughout the episode, even as Atlantis makes its last action-fuelled stand against the Wraith, an atmosphere of energy and tension that was also felt on set during filming.

"That was just a crazy shoot," recalls Rainbow Sun Francks. "It seemed like every day there was everything to do, like we shot a whole script every day. There were so many new people coming in with the whole Earth entourage arriving. For Ford on an individual level, it showed his military side coming out once again, because as soon as

Everett comes in, Ford is prepping him on tactical positions. It's not Sheppard in there, it's Ford, and that was pretty cool for Ford because he's the best guy to talk to about this — about what weapons he has and what's going on. For the audience it shows that he is still a military man — as close as he has become with his friends, he still has to be under that chain of command."

This conflict between military duty and civilian camaraderie made for a nice moment between the two characters, as Higginson remembers, though the scene didn't make the episode's final cut. "Ford and I had this lovely thing with just me meeting his eyes," recalls the actress. "He was the only one that just gave up — and he had no choice, he was military, this was a commanding officer. But he threw me this look that just broke my heart, which was almost both guilt and traitor at the same time."

Sheppard: ...if you cut Dr Weir out of the loop, you'll only alienate the people whose trust and respect she's earned. Which is everyone on the base. Including me.

As Ford, Francks also got to perform a heavy chunk of action in his last episode as a series regular, thanks largely to the ordinance built by Bridget McGuire and the production design team. "We built the rail gun for that episode, that gun that we're firing from the balcony. All the boys got excited about that!" laughs McGuire. "We made it interactive — it spun around and the barrel moved up and down and there were lots of buttons and a screen on it, so everybody loved that one! We looked at references on the Internet to rail guns and other large mobile guns, and sort of combined them all and made it up. It's just pretend, but based on real things so that it looks like something that might work. It's not complete whimsy, it's designed to look like something that could be real."

For Elizabeth Weir, the action of 'The Siege' part two led to several struggles of both a personal and professional nature. On the one hand, she got to exercise her considerable diplomatic skills in persuading the Genii to give up their warhead — and on the other it led to the most direct example of her commanding men to their deaths, as Sheppard boarded the doomed puddle-jumper. Something, the actress feels, that Weir could never have done during her early days in the Pegasus Galaxy.

"I think she would have fought it tooth and nail and said, 'We'll all go down together but I won't send any person to their deaths,'" the actress reflects, "but I think she'd learned not to do that. And also, it was his suggestion. I don't think she would have ordered him to do it, but he suggested it. He would have done it regardless, and she knew that about him too, and thought, 'How much control do I have here, and how much choice do we have? We're all going to die. So if he can maybe save us and is willing to and is going to do it, then I give him my blessing and send him off with my respect.'" Å

MAJOR JOHN SHEPPARD

"Don't take on an alien armada single-handedly. Understood."

"I had never seen *Stargate SG-1*," explains Joe Flanigan of his first introduction to the character of John Sheppard and the *Stargate* universe. "So I wasn't quite sure what the vibe was. I didn't realize that they had a self-deprecating quality." As a result, the actor says that he wasn't quite sure how to take the apparent deadpan surety and heroism of the character. "It read kind of 'on-the-nose'. I look at actors who are in action films, and the ones that tend to be interesting are the ones that aren't as cocksure. You get somebody like Stallone, there's not a minute of vulnerability — he just knows he's going to survive, and I was definitely not interested in that," Flanigan continues, highlighting his concerns. "Then, as I talked to the executive producers they said, 'Well, it's not actually quite like that. We want to have enough sarcasm that it lightens, but doesn't diminish, the material.' They were looking for that fine line — and then it became interesting, because until then I didn't know what the show was. I liked the idea of approaching the character from the standpoint of, 'He's screwed up before, he could screw up again.' He's not entirely sure whether this thing is going to work out or not. They liked that choice too, so it was great."

Flanigan's previous acting background in television had been in hard-hitting drama films and series such as *CSI: Miami* and the supernaturally-oriented *Profiler*. The actor had never previously had a role in the science fiction genre. With his casting as Major Sheppard, the actor admits that he was immediately thrust into a completely different television style, which was hard to adjust to. His first introduction to the difference between science fiction and Earth-based drama came in the two-part pilot episode, 'Rising'.

"He's kind of a by-stander in 'Rising'. That was a conscious choice they made, not to feature the character, not to make him so dominant that it would be obvious that he'd emerge as a hero. I was initially a little surprised, because I did think they were going to feature this character a little more, and that we were going to see this from his point of view. So I was surprised when I saw the first cut, because they didn't want to do it that way. They wanted to start in an ensemble pattern, and let the audience guess whether this character was going to become important or not. I knew this guy became the hero of the show, but it wasn't apparent to me in the first three quarters of the pilot. We went to wider shots of the set and the principles, as opposed to some of the coverage and close-up shots that I had planned for. But I came from a different place. A lot of the dramas I shot in Hollywood, they do really tight, close-up shots of you —

that's the style that a lot of dramas go for. But this is sci-fi, and sci-fi is on a bigger scale. So it was hard to adjust to. If you shoot *CSI: Miami* and you're on a super-wide angle like we were [for 'Rising'], a lot of the performances just won't read on screen."

Despite his surprise at the time, looking back the actor is happy that Brad Wright and Robert C. Cooper made the choices they did for the introduction of John Sheppard: "What you're seeing is a character in the background coming to the foreground. It was a more interesting arc. In retrospect, I realize that I didn't know *anything* about science fiction, and these guys had been around the block a number of times!"

The actor also puts his initial misgivings down to the cynicism he had developed over years of disappointment in the television industry: "I had unfortunately grown a little skeptical about a lot of things, having done a lot of shows and a lot of pilots. I had learned not to listen to executives, producers or studios, because 'nobody knows anything'. While you're shooting it they say it's the greatest thing in the world and it's going to be big, and then you discover the pilot isn't even going to make it to a series. That was the experience that I had come from, so I suspended my judgment and decided to wait and see what the outcome was. It wasn't until I actually saw the final cut of the show I thought to myself, 'Now, that's really exciting!' I'm not a science fiction aficionado, but I would say 'Rising' was a great show. So I was hoping that [the audience] would like it too — and we were lucky that they did." Å

PROGRESS REPORT
Major John Sheppard

John Sheppard has come a long way during this first year in the Pegasus Galaxy. I know he was reluctant to come with us at first, but once agreeing to join the expedition he never once showed any signs of being anything less than one hundred percent committed to doing the best job he could. I suspect that, despite the tragic circumstances that necessitated it, his de facto appointment as head of military operations in Atlantis has helped him focus himself somehow. He accepted the responsibility with grace and a cool head — and as for the supposed 'black mark' on his official record back home, I don't think the sharing of leadership between a civilian and a military officer would have gone so well had anyone else been in his shoes. He is an excellent tactician and strategist, is very good at making the most of what we have available, and has saved the lives of everyone in the city on more than one occasion, even when his own life has been threatened.

I confess that there have been moments where I have been less impressed with his manner. He has overruled me more than once, and in several cases if he had thought a little bit more about

what he was doing, or consulted me before making a decision off world, our lives here would have been made a little easier. That does make me apprehensive of the future, but at the same time I do understand his actions, and I can also see that his intentions were not to undermine my authority, but to help preserve the safety of our community. I am also convinced that had any other officer been in his shoes, these incidents would have been far more frequent. These factors mitigate his behavior in my mind, and make me confident that we can continue to work together, perhaps even more harmoniously. Now, as we in Atlantis prepare to face our biggest challenge so far, I know there is no one I would prefer managing our safety.

— **Dr Elizabeth Weir**

DR ELIZABETH WEIR

"This chair controls the most powerful weapons known to human-kind — I'm afraid of the thing."

For actress Torri Higginson, who would go on to perfect her second 'incarnation', Dr Elizabeth Weir was immediately striking. "I liked her," says the actress simply, recalling her first thoughts of the character that she would go on to make her own so successfully. "Before the auditions, you're not given an entire script, you're just given ten pages, so you try to compile a character out of very bare bones. But I immediately liked her. There was a scene that we actually ended up not changing much for the first episode, between Sheppard and myself, and we're just kind of challenging each other. I thought that she was strong, but not overbearing. She's still a woman but she has a quiet strength, and that comes through — her diplomacy. I got that immediately. That was how I perceived her based on those first sides [of script]."

At the time, Higginson had no idea that she was coming in to replace Jessica Stein, who had previously introduced Weir's character in the conclusion of *Stargate SG-1*'s seventh season. "I wasn't aware of the fact that the character had been 'born' by another actor," she explains. "I was then offered the job and accepted, and it was only at that point that I found out!

"They showed me the video," recalls Higginson, admitting that the discovery of another Weir caused her quite a lot of concern, "and I panicked a bit, because [Stein] had dealt with her very differently than I did. I found it to be a very different take on the character. But through conversations with Brad Wright and Martin Wood, they reassured me and said that they had liked what they'd seen in the auditions, and that I should trust my instincts and go with that. So I did!"

Weir's involvement in the *Stargate SG-1* universe also meant that the actress had to finish up the character's involvement with the SGC before the diplomat could embark on the Atlantis expedition. "What was interesting was that we started shooting the pilot of *Stargate: Atlantis* before I was needed on *Stargate SG-1*," Higginson reveals. "'Rising' was about a fourteen or fifteen day shoot because we shot two episodes as one, but halfway through that I went over to *Stargate SG-1*. So I was then shooting them both at the same time. It was kind of hectic, but it was a nice way to be thrown into it, because I was too busy to worry too much," laughs the actress. "You just had to get down to it, know your lines and remember what set you were on! It didn't give me the chance to be the neurotic actor that I would probably like to be, given the chance! So that was nice, and those guys were amazing. Michael Shanks and the others were just incredibly welcoming and funny and warm. They made it just seem very

exciting to be a part of."

Higginson also appreciates the extra time that appearing as Weir in *Stargate SG-1* afforded her in creating her vision of the character. "At the beginning of this science fiction series," says the actress, who has plenty of experience in the genre, "you're dealing with introducing an entirely new galaxy, introducing new people and the Wraith — you're having to explain a lot, so it wasn't so much about personalities [of the characters]. Everyone was just establishing the world that we were in. So that's what was so important about doing *Stargate SG-1*. That gave me a chance to get to know who she was a bit, because that was on Earth, and it gave me a chance to just be vulnerable, and be human."

It is this human side of Weir that Higginson continued to bring to the fore throughout *Stargate: Atlantis*' first year on air. The actress admits, however, that to begin with, she wished the exploration of that aspect of her character was happening at a greater pace. "All actors love action and emotional delving. My character isn't an action character, so as an actor you always go, 'Oh, there should have been more emotion. Oh, there should have been a weepy goodbye with her dog!'" explains Higginson, using the expedition's departure from Earth as an example. "You want to show your chops and do all that kind of stuff — there's that natural egotism where you think, 'It would have been fun to be doing that.' But what you learn in a series is that to be able to fill one season, let alone maybe eight or nine, you can't blow it all in the first episode. I actually didn't fully grasp that until about episode five or six. All of a sudden, instead of getting frustrated with not being able to get as emotional or as personal as I'd like, to show what I could do as an actor and to show what I liked about this character, I finally got excited with thinking, 'This is wonderful, because we're creating a slow arc that we can develop, and introduce new things over the years.' And that's actually much more detailed, and much more subtle." Å

PROGRESS REPORT
Dr Elizabeth Weir

Assessing one's own progress under changing situations can be hard, but I feel it is a useful tool to understanding oneself, particularly in circumstances such as these. And, since I am including progress reports for the other key members of my team here in this transmission, I felt it only just that I try to do the same for myself.

I must confess that this sort of journey was not something I could ever have envisioned experiencing. Even following my introduction to the notion of space travel and other races, my sensibilities and personal philosophy have remained rooted in understanding humanity, and I suppose the best way to describe my personal progress over the past year is in terms of what more I have learnt about the human condition.

The resilience and perseverance of those around me here is constantly astounding. We have come so far from home, have been so isolated from what is familiar, and yet each of us has continued to grow. I, myself, have had to come to terms with the fact that there may be sentient species in existence that simply cannot be negotiated with. I managed to reason — in some ways, anyway — with the Goa'uld, but from what I see and hear about the Wraith, it is likely that there is no peaceful solution to the threat they bring. And as much as this saddens me, as much as it makes me reassess my own view of the universe,

it has also taught me to rely on the judgment of the military members of my team far more than I may have done in the past. This journey has been exhilarating, terrifying and at times heartbreaking, but despite what we face now, I am glad — proud — to be experiencing it with these people.

— **Dr Elizabeth Weir**

TEYLA EMMAGAN

"If the Wraith have never touched your world, you should go back there."

"Teyla is a very deep character. She's quite spiritual, I think — and I don't mean religious. I just think she has a deep connection with life,".says actress Rachel Luttrell of her character who, over the course of the first year of *Stargate: Atlantis*, became an invaluable part of Major Sheppard's team.

It's hard to imagine the show had she been absent — but, as Luttrell reveals, *Stargate: Atlantis* very nearly did go ahead without her! "It was the beginning of pilot season," she explains, "where the studios generate piles of new shows. *Stargate: Atlantis* was my very first pilot audition of the season, and I had actually been telling friends and family that I wanted to take a little break from acting. I thought maybe I'd travel, or study something completely different. So it's kind of amusing in a way that the very first pilot that I auditioned for ended up being this wonderful thing! I don't want to sound absurd, but I did feel like it was touched with some sort of divine intervention, because from the moment I stepped into the room with the first casting agent, it was bizarrely golden. They were just immediately trying to get me the job," the actress laughs. "I wasn't wearing the appropriate clothes and she said, 'Okay, so come back and wear something like this, and do this…' From that very moment, I felt like I was being gently nudged along."

As the casting agents continued to be impressed with Luttrell's performances in the auditions, she neared the next level of auditions — in front of the studio network representatives. Despite the pressures at this kind of audition, the actress was still confident, and with good cause: "Before I actually did the network test, the casting agents told my representatives that if I just did the same thing again, it was mine. The test went fantastically well — ridiculously well. I tested with Joe, who had already got the part of Sheppard, and he came out afterwards and gave me a huge hug and said, 'They love you, it's yours,' and I had network executives coming out and shaking my hand. It was just amazing. But then I found out that actually, I *hadn't* got the job!"

In a sudden change of heart, the actress's agent discovered that despite their happiness with her performance in auditions, the network had decided that she wasn't right for the role. "I moved on, I started to prepare for other shows, and I was starting to get close to other parts," says Luttrell. "Then, out of the blue, about a week after hearing that the job was no longer mine, I had a phone call from my agent who said, 'Okay Rachel, they called back and they've actually been fighting for you this whole time, and the part is yours — but they want you there in twelve hours!'" Luttrell laughs again, remembering that hectic time. "It was the craziest thing. It went from this incredible, focused period of trying to get the job and feeling like it was mine, to

then finding out that I didn't get the job and grieving and moving on — and then, lo and behold, it came through! I literally had a night to put my things together and come up to Vancouver. We started shooting four days after I arrived, and I hadn't even read the script yet. It was quite a crazy period!"

Despite the rushed start to the season, the actress really enjoyed making the character her own over the course of the first year. "When I was auditioning, I really felt like I knew who this person was. I had a good grasp on who Teyla was, at least from my perspective, and thankfully that's what the writers ended up using," she laughs. "Characters slowly reveal themselves to you as an actor, and I just felt a really strong connection towards her when I first read the sides that were offered in the audition process. But once I'd finally got the script, and after our first table-read, we were shooting virtually the next day. I was really flying by the seat of my pants and going by gut instinct. Thankfully, Martin Wood, who directed our pilot and a lot of our subsequent shows this past season, was fantastic in terms of nudging me along and supporting my instincts."

One distinct aspect to Teyla's character that has been very evident during the first season is her fighting skills. For Luttrell, developing this side of her character didn't only mean going back to her training as a dancer, but also learning something entirely new. "I'm loving the whole physical aspect of Teyla," the actress enthuses. "I just thought it would be great to get a job that required me to learn a new physical skill, and this is certainly that! I really do enjoy that part of her.

"Something else that's interesting about Teyla is that she's human, but she's not from Earth. That presents a very unique challenge for me in portraying her, because although she will react to certain things in the same way that you or I would, there has to be something that sets her apart, because her point of reference is completely different. It's an interesting journey for me. I am also quite excited about pursuing the various relationships with the other characters. That's what's fun about a series, there are just so many opportunities." Å

PROGRESS REPORT
Teyla Emmagan

Though Teyla does not answer to Earth's governmental systems, I wanted to include a word about her here, so that the SGC can understand what an integral part of our team she has become. When we first came to the Pegasus Galaxy, we were friendless and thus, despite our weapons and technology, vulnerable. Teyla was the first native of this place to offer her hand in friendship, and she has since assisted Major Sheppard and myself in countless issues peculiar to this galaxy. Without Teyla and her people, we would have found out about the Wraith in a much harder way, and our first encounter with this dread enemy could have been our last.

Since deciding that she could best provide for the future of her people by remaining with Major Sheppard's team, Teyla has put herself in danger on our behalf many times. She is a fearless warrior, never thinking of herself but always thinking of others — and indeed, it was thanks to her prowess in this area that we managed to capture our first Wraith prisoner. Her knowledge of planets in Pegasus has allowed us to venture forth with more certainty than most explorers, which has only enriched our experience here, and in most cases, smoothed the way for peaceful communication with other races.

It would be a mistake to write Teyla and her people off as a non-industrial, unevolved society. Though for the past few centuries they have preferred to live as an agrarian, nomadic community to avoid the Wraith, their civilization was once very technologically advanced. To my mind, the fact

that the Athosians can exhibit such a spiritual nature in the face of such adversity is testament to their evolved state. In future, I would like to have the opportunity to discuss Teyla's culture with her further, since I feel there is much to be learned from their way of life.

— **Dr Elizabeth Weir**

LIEUTENANT AIDEN FORD

"It's a ship. It goes through the gate. Gateship One!"

"I think he's just excited," says Rainbow Sun Francks, of Aiden Ford. "He's really gung ho about going into action — he's very headstrong in that respect. I think that can be a good thing and a bad thing, but it's always good for the character. He's always ready. When Sheppard says something like, 'I'm in trouble,' he's always ready — 'Let's go! You heard him, let's go! He's in trouble!' That's his mentality — whatever's happening, let's be a part of it if we can. Sometimes he doesn't take into account that he could be running into danger," the actor laughs, "and that's why he's a First Lieutenant, and not the Major!"

Coming from an athletic background of breakdancing and a whole family of actors, Francks has the same frenetic energy as his character. Clearly thrilled to be a part of the *Stargate: Atlantis* universe, the young actor — just twenty-four years old when cast as Lieutenant Aiden Ford — feels that the first season of the show was as much of a learning experience for him as it was for Ford. For a start, though he had experienced working in feature films, *Stargate: Atlantis* was the first time Francks had encountered the pressures of working on a television series.

"In contrast to film it's been excruciatingly painful at times, but a nurturing experience overall," he laughs. "The advantage is that I get to act every day, so I get to grow every day: not only acting-wise, but also in having a character progress from the pilot to the end of the first season. It's great in that respect, because in a film you have to build your character right away, and little subtleties go unnoticed. I can do it as I go along, so that's been a lot of fun."

Just as Francks gradually found his feet as Ford, so too the Lieutenant gradually began to settle into his role within the Atlantis expedition team. The actor feels that most of his character's growth in season one was down to adjusting to the peculiar situation of being in the Pegasus Galaxy itself. "Mostly he's building relationships with the other characters, as far as everyone coming together and no one knowing each other," Francks explains. "Ending up stranded in another galaxy, he's had to deal with everyone's intricacies — being a marine and having to deal with a lot of civilians who may not think the same way as him. He's started to let down his guard a little bit and show more of a sense of humor, and is actually treating these people around him as his family. And he's the young guy so he's still learning about life, too. Having a character like McKay always ragging on you is a lot of fun too," he laughs. "There's a lot to learn from people like David Hewlett, who's just an incredible actor, and a great friend now."

As the primary weapons expert in Atlantis, Ford's role is necessarily one of action — and as the season progressed Francks found himself doing a lot more than simply

LIEUTENANT AIDEN FORD

looking down the barrel of a gun! "I've done all my own stunts. Except for one in the pilot, everything Aiden's done has been me," says Francks happily. "James Bamford, who is our stunt coordinator, and also Brad Wright, have been very nice in letting me put myself in harm's way now and then! I've been jumping around and going through training, learning different special ops and different ways of taking guys down, and actually doing it. That's been a lot of fun. Both Rachel and I have been really taking that into our characters, and it's been great for me. Especially because in the first season, being the youngest and being the second in command in this group, I'm always there but I don't always have a lot to say. But when it comes to action, I can use the fact that I have my youth; I can throw my body around. I only have it for so long, so I'd better use it now!"

One of the most complicated pieces of action work Francks participated in during the first season was in 'The Brotherhood', for a sequence where Ford was without the protection of his precious P-90. "I did my first hand-to-hand stuff in 'The Brotherhood', when we get trapped by the Genii. There's a 290lb guy who I had taken down earlier and he knocked me out, and so I sort of have a vendetta against him. I run straight at him, wrap my arm around him, wrap this leg around him, wrap this arm around him, wrap his arm around his neck, use all of my body weight against him upside down, flip him over me, break his arm, take his gun..." Francks laughs, "and a month on, I was actually *still* recovering from that! We practiced it probably a dozen times — it wasn't very many. I didn't have very much time to learn it, but that's where me being an athlete and dancing my whole life helps. The basic coordination is all a dance, so if you have coordination you can get it, if you don't have coordination it will take you a lot longer."

All in all, the first season has been a blast for the young actor. "It's been an experience of a lifetime, the best time I've had in a long time," he says. "It's definitely my favorite work experience thus far. I'm happy to come to work, and that's something that we can't all say." Å

PROGRESS REPORT
Lieutenant Aiden Ford

I've rarely met a young man more enthusiastic and full of zest for life than Lieutenant Ford, as evidenced by his extraordinary dedication in leaving behind his family and friends to embark on this journey into the unknown with us. However, despite his youth and exuberance, Ford also exhibits a maturity that few his age could pretend to equal. He has dedicated himself to learning all there is to know about the Wraith weapons systems we have encountered, knowledge that is sure to stand us in good stead as we face down the approaching armada. He has shown fierce loyalty to his fellow team members, even putting himself in jeopardy to join Sheppard in an attempt to rescue Colonel Sumner, a mission that I must confess I was not eager to allow. It scares me that I am responsible for the wellbeing of one so young, particularly when I am faced with the reality of sending him out into this unknown galaxy to confront such a fearsome enemy. Yet he has never once shirked his responsibilities, and in my mind will, in the future, be ready for many more. He has the capacity to be a great leader of men, something I hope is apparent from the mission

reports we have included with this transmission, and which I hope the military establishment at the SGC will take into close consideration. I would like to think that Lieutenant Ford's truly admirable actions throughout this first year will earn him the right to pursue his career as he would wish, with all help from the military chain of command. I would certainly be happy to personally stand witness to his abilities.

— **Dr Elizabeth Weir**

DR RODNEY MCKAY

"How could I possibly know that? What am I? Answer Man?"

"I am having the best time of my life," says David Hewlett of his role as the irascible Dr Rodney McKay. "I am the biggest sci-fi geek — I *love* this stuff. My friends and I used to make these little mutant horror films on 8mm film when I was a kid, so I've been doing this forever — and now I get paid for it!"

Born and raised in Britain on a healthy science fiction television diet of *Doctor Who*, the actor found himself gravitating towards roles that reminded him of his earliest memories, appearing in films such as *Cube* and *Cypher* before joining the cast of *Stargate: Atlantis*. "*Doctor Who* was a huge thing for me," says Hewlett. "Growing up I was like, 'I want to be a Time Lord and travel the galaxy like Doctor Who, but I can't be, so can I pretend to be one instead?' And this job is very similar to that: I get to go through the gate and explore new worlds — and all of them are near Vancouver," he jokes.

Of all the characters in *Stargate: Atlantis*, McKay was the last and yet also the most natural choice to join the expedition team. Since the character had already appeared in three episodes of *Stargate SG-1*, his cranky, superior manner was well established, and the writers knew how to write for Hewlett's acting sensibilities. Despite all those factors, however, Hewlett reports that the offer of a regular role on *Stargate: Atlantis* was still a huge shock. "I heard the show was going, and had put out some tentacles, because I thought, 'Great, maybe McKay can come back for a couple of episodes.'" The actor laughs, "I never thought it would be for all of them!"

Hewlett has relished the opportunity to expand on the character that he had previously only played as a guest star. "I just came in for one guest star appearance, which then turned into three," he says of *Stargate SG-1*. "I just had so much fun, and they *let* me have fun. At the time I never would have thought of playing him continually. But then when he came back for two more, I thought, 'This guy's cooler than I thought he would be.' It's funny, because as a guest star you get to be a jerk, just because you don't have to sustain anything. But what's great about this is that I *still* get to be a jerk! McKay isn't that different — there are some changes, there is some softening, but only because you see him regularly. You definitely get some insight into the little mushy marshmallow guy behind all the sarcasm, but that's just part of seeing someone on a day-to-day basis. I still get to be the guy at the front of the class who's always got the answer. The one who is convinced everyone is an idiot, and luckily is smart enough to back it up most of the time."

The character has also learnt a few new skills since his arrival in the Pegasus Galaxy, which has been a surprise not only for McKay, but also for Hewlett. The highlight of the first season was "being handed a P-90!" Hewlett laughs. "I said, 'You're joking,

right? I'm going to have to fire this?' I mean, I know that's every actor's dream, but I was just so surprised when they did that! I originally saw McKay as the guy behind the computer, you know, snarky as always — 'snarkastic', as the term seems to be now — filling everyone in on the technical details. And then all of a sudden we're doing the show and I'm out in the field and shooting Wraith and still being snarkastic!"

The actor is also relieved that although McKay's manner gives rise to plenty of comedic moments, the character hasn't turned into the show's standard outlet for comic relief. "I definitely get to lighten things up, but what's nice is that everyone's got a good sense of humor. The beauty of *Stargate SG-1*, that has come through very strongly with *Stargate: Atlantis*, is the comedy. The whole point of this is that it's contemporary people dealing with science fiction. How would normal people deal with these very creepy-looking creatures? In life, things are funny. People find things funny that are inappropriate, people find things funny when they're in peril... The thing to avoid is the audience thinking it's going to be a funny scene whenever McKay shows up. So what's nice about this is, yes, I get to be funny, but I also get to guide storylines, and panic, and act. It's so nice to be able to do that."

Hewlett puts the strong comedy aspect of both *Stargate SG-1* and *Stargate: Atlantis* down to the team behind each show. "These parts come along but they are few and far between, especially with a show like this, where the producers also write the show. This is their baby, and it shows. The thing is," the actor says, laughing, "and they might be offended by this — if Brad Wright and Robert Cooper were to morph into somebody together, it would be McKay! They are brilliant, they are sarcastic, they enjoy themselves and they enjoy the repartee. We had a meal the other day, and Robert was at the end of the table making me laugh. I was thinking, 'That's McKay, right there!' When I go home for the holidays I miss having an answer for everything, because McKay's always got something smart to say, and I don't!" Å

PROGRESS REPORT
Dr Rodney McKay

Anything that I have to say professionally about Dr McKay will pale into insignificance against the amazing feats of science and ingenuity he has performed in Atlantis. We came to this galaxy knowing precious little about what we would find, and yet through the endeavors of Dr McKay and the team under his guidance, we have learned to operate most of its systems, and have overcome countless difficulties caused by our power shortage problem. He has also acquired new skills far outside the scope of his profession — learning to use a weapon in self-defense being among them. I believe that he is now an integral part of Major Sheppard's team, not only because of his scientific prowess but also because of his growing proficiency in this area.

On a personal level, though I think Rodney will always be something of an abrasive personality, I have seen him mellow slightly during this year. Perhaps it is the isolation and the small size of our community, but I can see that others have warmed to him, and in his own way he has become more closely involved with the team. He has started the first Pegasus Galaxy chapter of Mensa, and while I doubt that this will broaden his relationships with most members of the expedition, it does mean he has like-minds to spar with.

Rodney has had his fair share of bad circumstances to deal with, including the death of his close colleague Dr Gaul at Wraith hands, and several other colleagues to a nanite infection. I am also sure that the challenge of keeping Atlantis running — which, while not singularly Rodney's responsibility, must rest heavily on his shoulders at all times — causes its own degree of stress. Of course I have not had this confirmed in an official capacity, but it is my hope that he is taking advantage of the psychological help offered by Dr Heightmeyer, who has helped us all to cope with these strange new surroundings and the demands exerted by them.

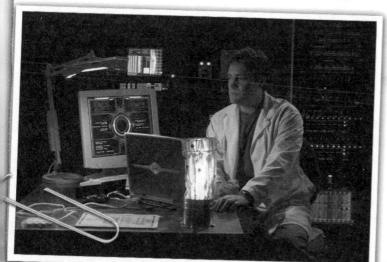

— **Dr Elizabeth Weir**

DR CARSON BECKETT

"You don't understand. I break things like this!"

Although not listed as a regular member of the *Stargate: Atlantis* cast until the beginning of season two, Paul McGillion made such an immediate impression as Dr Carson Beckett that he was soon indispensable, not only to the fans but also to the show's producers. McGillion had really made the character his own right from his first audition, where the actor, whose own accent is North American, decided to use his family's Scottish roots as the basis for Beckett's personality, not to mention his distinctive Gaelic twang.

"It's fun to play a Scottish character," he laughs. "I was born in Scotland, in Paisley. When I initially read for the character he wasn't Scottish. It was just that they wanted an international flavor to the character and that's what I came up with — Scottish. Fortunately that went my way!"

Over the course of the season, McGillion feels that the character really began to expand, certainly far beyond what he had originally expected: "Beckett initially wasn't as prevalent as he is now, and so I think the character has really grown in a lot of ways. Initially it was only going to be a recurring character and we didn't know where he was going to fit in, and as it turns out I've been in a lot of episodes. I've had a great opportunity to play a lot comically and also dramatically, particularly in 'Poisoning the Well'. It was great to flesh out the character and to show that emotional side. So I've been very fortunate — the fans seemed to be responding to the character and as a result, he was written in more."

Even though when the actor first took the role of Beckett he hadn't bargained on having to slip into the Scottish brogue quite so often and for so long, McGillion reports that he doesn't find keeping up the doctor's accent too much of a challenge, though he does often get a second opinion on how he should deliver a line.

"I don't have problems keeping the accent up, I just want to make sure that it's understandable for a lot of people," he says. "I could do one a lot thicker if I wanted to, but it's getting an accent that is palatable for all audiences. So I tend to slow my dialogue down a little bit so that it's understandable. Certain words are said differently in a Scottish accent than in a North American accent, so when I read it to myself I'll work at it and break it down with the accent. I've got a lot of Scottish friends and my parents, of course, so I call them up and ask them about stuff. I have no problem doing that, and if I can get better, I'm keen to do that. I'm learning too, and when you're dealing with that amount of dialogue it's best to run it by somebody who's got a good ear for the accent."

Hearing the accent on screen is something that McGillion really enjoys, and he feels, too, that it really adds to *Stargate: Atlantis*' overall tone and appeal: "I think the

DR CARSON BECKETT

sensibility of the Scots brings a nice flavor to the cast. We also have a Czech character, Zelenka, who has been developed more too, and David Nykl who plays him is fantastic. It really broadens the show."

McGillion's increased screen time in the first year also meant more opportunity to expand on the character's comic potential. Some of that comedy aspect of Beckett that the actor relished so much came from the doctor's sparring with David Hewlett's Rodney McKay, which he points to as one of the most enjoyable aspects of his first year on the show.

"We do have some great moments but we didn't actually get to work together that much, and hopefully we'll get to do more," McGillion enthuses. "I would like to see David and I have an episode together, maybe where we're trapped somewhere and can have a lot of witty repartee — or hopefully that would be the case! It seems that most of the time that we are both on, we carry most of the dialogue so they separate us in the scripts, but David and I really enjoy working with each other. At least, that's what I'm saying," says the actor with a shout of laughter. "Hopefully he'll say the same!"

While the actors enjoy working together and are great friends, the two characters' relationship isn't always as clear-cut. "I'm the head of Medicine and he's the head of Science, and we have that kind of Spock-McCoy love-hate relationship," says McGillion, laughing again as he recalls the times the two characters have met on screen. "I think Beckett would secretly consider Rodney to be his best friend, but he'd never want him to know that!"

Despite Beckett's somewhat timid nature, the doctor did find himself in the thick of the action several times during *Stargate: Atlantis'* first year, which included going off-world, brandishing a weapon and learning to fly a puddle-jumper.

"I love this character, I love the way it's going. Any sort of adventures I can go on [as Beckett] are great as an actor. I love being in a lab, too, analyzing the Wraith and that sort of thing, and any time you can bring a human side to the character is great too. The first season did a great job of fleshing out the characters. We're very fortunate, because we're following on the tail of *Stargate SG-1*, a terrific show. The executive producers, Brad Wright, Robert C. Cooper and John Smith knew how to handle the production — they've done it for so many years — and we just had to follow their lead and trust it. The crew is fantastic, and I think the cast really gelled. We get along very well, and it shows on screen." Å

PROGRESS REPORT
Dr Carson Beckett

Of all the members who joined the Atlantis expedition, I think the one who has shown the most striking personal progress over this past year has to be Dr Beckett. I do not need to vouch for his professional expertise, which has continued in the Pegasus Galaxy, just as on Earth, at a level of unmatched genius which this expedition has found invaluable. His initial work on isolating the Ancient gene has since enabled him to produce a revolutionary gene therapy that can reactivate this dormant DNA component in most humans. This side of him was never in question when I picked him for this mission. Rather, my concerns about Carson were with regards to his rather timid disposition, and it is here that the doctor is almost unrecognizable. Though he is always still reluctant to allow himself to be relied upon outside the strict confines of his laboratory, our stay in the Pegasus Galaxy has seen him performing remarkable feats of courage. Always suspicious of using his own natural ability with Ancient technology, Carson has nonetheless learned to fly the Ancient ships that we have nicknamed the puddle-jumpers. He has used the Stargate to travel to many planets, and has on numerous occasions defended Atlantis with his own life. I am pleased to say now that though many questioned whether Dr Beckett would survive the mental stresses of the Pegasus Galaxy, I would not have traded his presence here with us for anyone else in his field. And, though he may never admit it, I think that despite the mortal danger we now find ourselves in, given the opportunity to change his decision, Carson would still choose to join us.

— **Dr Elizabeth Weir**

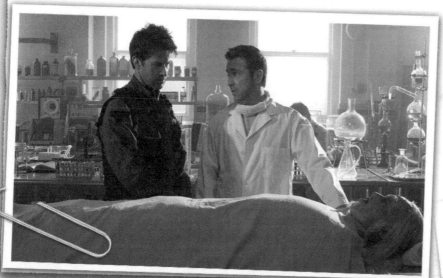

RECURRING CAST

Though not usually on set every day, actors who portray supporting and recurring roles provide a show's essential background, familiar faces that give a series depth as it progresses. *Stargate SG-1* frequently manages to cast actors for recurring roles who fit so well into the workings of the production that they return season after season. Sometimes these actors are so ideal that they find their characters being written in for terms far longer than the usual recurring role. Take David Hewlett, who, after playing McKay for two episodes in *Stargate SG-1*, was picked to return as a regular in *Stargate: Atlantis*. Similarly, since it's very first episode, when genre veteran Robert Patrick took a guest starring role as Colonel Sumner, *Stargate: Atlantis* has attracted some of the finest supporting cast in any current show. And, as the series continues, it's certain that some of these will return too.

You may not recognize **James Lafazanos** outside of the roles he played during the first year of *Stargate: Atlantis*, since without the long, straggly hair, the pointed, rotting teeth and the formidable leather costume, he looks pretty normal! First brought on to the show to play the Male Wraith in 'Rising' part two, the statuesque actor soon found that he had carved a niche for himself in the expanding *Stargate: Atlantis* mythology, and ended up returning to the show a total of six times in its first year to play various Wraith characters, including 'Steve' and 'Bob'.

"I like to give a different vibe to each one," the actor says regarding his Wraith roles. "There are obviously characteristics that they all share, in that they're energy-thirsty vampires," he adds, laughing, "but between Steve and the character from 'The Defiant One' and 'The Siege', I think I gave them all a unique spin. They looked different, but I also gave them a personality, a character that said what their life was about. Particularly Bob in 'The Siege' — he was kind of a 'bounty hunter' Wraith. Whenever I was doing the lines for that one I felt this whole 'Dirty Harry' thing coming out of me! He was a no-bull taking Wraith who had seen more than most. But there's definitely room for even stronger characterization of the Wraith."

For Lafazanos, undergoing prosthetic make-up to play the male Wraith in 'Rising' was a new experience, yet he found it surprisingly easy to adjust, despite the odd moment of discomfort. "I went in to have a mold done, the arms, head and neck — and the first time they molded my arm I pulled it out and ripped off half my arm hair!" laughs the actor, remembering the pain with good humor. "It's an interesting process. The guys that do my make-up are great and they make it really easy. I sit there for a couple of hours every morning and we just joke to pass the time."

The Wraith went through several design changes during the filming of 'Rising', as the production discovered and solved problems with some of the prosthetic pieces, as Lafazanos reveals: "Initially they had 'gloves' for me too — they were a bit difficult to use outside of filming. Then they painted my hands and put on nails, but they had an issue with the nails because they were falling off all the time… sometimes it can be tedious, but it's a laugh really. You've got to take it in your stride and smile about it. And I tend to ham it up too, when I'm in costume. It gives me more of an excuse to be funny!"

Though Lafazanos has no problem acting in the heavy make-up and costume required to make the Wraith so terrifying, he occasionally does still make the most of other people's reactions to his appearance off-camera! "I just enjoy other people's first reactions now," he says mischievously. "I play with that and that's fun! People are great on set, they are really awesome, and once people are around me for a while then the make-up is nothing. They catch my vibe beyond the character and I usually end up joking around with a lot of the crew in between takes. But it

Below: Lafazanos as the Wraith Bob in 'The Siege'.

can be alarming for some people," he laughs. "I think there are certain members of the cast that still don't know how to take me. They smile, but kind of give me a weird look at the same time!"

South African-born actor **Craig Veroni** made a total of nine appearances as Peter Grodin before his brave yet untimely demise in 'The Siege' part one. Having emigrated to Canada at the age of eight, and now living in Vancouver, the actor has appeared in numerous series and films, including post-apocalyptic drama *Dark Angel*,

Below: Veroni as Peter Grodin, with Weir.

short-lived monster fest *Special Unit 2* and the super-powered hit *Smallville*. Veroni is also no stranger to the *Stargate SG-1* universe, having appeared in the seventh season episode 'Grace'.

After working with director Martin Wood on *Jeremiah*, and having appeared in a seventh season episode of *Stargate SG-1* ('Revisions') **Christopher Heyerdahl** found himself with the opportunity to take part in *Stargate: Atlantis* from a very early point.

"I guess Martin felt that I was someone that he wanted to work with," says the softly-spoken Norwegian. "We had done something together on *Jeremiah* the year before, and we established a working relationship there, and then he got me in to do the *Stargate SG-1* episode. Then *Stargate: Atlantis* came up, so we started talking about the realities of what this character entailed, and where Halling could go in the development of the show. I certainly liked the possibilities that the character could bring to this gang of adventurers, and decided to jump on board with both feet."

Charged with introducing the audience to the first alien race they would meet in the Pegasus Galaxy, Heyerdahl was anxious that Halling's character be clearly defined. "I really needed to know for myself where this character was going to go," he explains. "It was pretty open-ended off the top, reading the pilot. I had lots of questions about who this guy was, and the producers' vision of where this character was going. They had very broad strokes at that time about what was going to happen with him, but he was definitely going to be a major element of the Athosian influence on these people."

Despite the initial uncertainty of what direction the character would move in, Heyerdahl liked what he read. "I got a chance to play a character that is a good role model, a good father, a strong, gentle man who is not afraid to show love to his son, and not afraid to protect his son," he says. "One of the first moments of the show is the fact that he throws his body in front of his son and his playmate, and is not afraid to lose his own life in front of these strange new people with their strange new weapons. That kind of strong sense of male character is always a good role model."

To say that actor **David Nykl** made the part of scientist Dr Zelenka his own is something of an understatement, particularly considering that when he read for the part, the character was significantly different. "Originally the character was meant to

Below: Heyerdahl as Halling, meeting Colonel Sumner.

be a Russian," explains the Czech-born actor. "He had a [different] name, but what the name was I don't remember! But I came in for the audition late in the afternoon and it was the scene from '38 Minutes', where Dr Zelenka and Weir are talking about fixing the puddle-jumper. It was the scene where he goes, 'Stop talking!' I had an old pair of reading glasses with me which were my own personal reading glasses, and I wore those to the audition. They had me read a couple of times and they asked me what my heritage was and I said that I was Czech. I found out a few days later that not only did I get the part, but that they had changed the name from the Russian doctor to Dr Zelenka. And the glasses became part of the character!"

Nykl's role in '38 Minutes' made such an impression that Zelenka, though originally intended to only appear in the show once, became a very popular semi-regular character: "When I did find out I would be coming back, they wrote a little bit into 'Suspicion', where McKay and I are in the jumper bay and the roof opens up. That part was written in when it was decided that they would try me out for another episode. I had already been working on the character, so it's just a building process from there on in."

The addition of Zelenka prompted a thrilled response from Czech viewers, who

Below: Nykl as Zelenka, with McKay, tries to figure out how to destroy the nanovirus in 'Hot Zone'.

were particularly pleased with the character's tendency to burst into his native language. "I switch from English to Czech very readily, I have full fluency," Nykl explains. "All of the little Czech ad-libs which the Czech fans are just loving, I do all of those myself. I'm very excited about the internationalism that *Atlantis* represents, so any opportunity to build that into the character is something that I welcome."

Netting baddie heavy-weight **Robert Davi** even before the show had aired and become a hit was quite a casting coup for the *Stargate: Atlantis* team. Davi provided arguably the first season's best and most menacing villain, Commander Acastus Kolya. Having appeared in numerous movies and television series, Davi's resume ranges from 007 adventure *License to Kill* and *Die Hard* with Bruce Willis to *Profiler*. In 2005 he also starred alongside *Stargate: Atlantis* guest star Leonar Varela ('Sanctuary') in *Gilgamesh*. Å

PRODUCTION DESIGN

BRIDGET MCGUIRE

D esigning the city of Atlantis was a very different proposition to designing Stargate Command. For a start, unlike at the SGC, *Stargate:
Atlantis'* sets would not be based around a military compound. It was
also, rather than being based on Earth surroundings, set millions of
miles away from Earthly influences, in the Pegasus Galaxy.

For Bridget McGuire, who was called upon to design and create the physical representation of Atlantis, it was a task that was more than a little challenging. "I really
didn't think that *Stargate: Atlantis* was going to go ahead [that] year," says the production designer, who already had eight years of experience with *Stargate SG-1* under her
talented belt. "We left at the end of the [*Stargate SG-1*] season with the idea that if they
hadn't made the decision to do it by that time — and that was back in October —
then it wasn't going to happen that year. Then I got a phone call from John Smith in
the middle of November. He wanted me to come in for a meeting, and then the next
day I was designing. That was a Thursday and on Monday I had the crew back in
here doing drawings! It was a lot of sets to design in a very short period of time."

Having been given what amounted to a pretty much blank slate, McGuire and her
team were building Atlantis from scratch. The actual inspiration for the shape of the
city, McGuire explains, came from the natural world, and the first inklings of the
design had already been seen in *Stargate SG-1*.

"The set that I did for 'Lost City' was the first Ancient structure that we had seen
that wasn't a ruin or an artifact," she says. "So for 'Lost City' I based the designs on
images seen through an electron microscope, which they use to look at snowflakes.
You get this very strange geometry and it looks very structural and architectural.
Then, when we went to do the standing set for *Stargate: Atlantis*, I stayed with basing
everything on triangles. So the whole set is mostly on those angles. You see almost no
circles other than the Stargate and the conference room, and the idea is that anything
that is circular is made by a machine, so the architecture of this space is angles."

McGuire's starting point for the sets that would become *Stargate: Atlantis'* hallmark,
however, was actually much more practical. "I always start with the layout of the
space so that I can work out how movement can flow from one area to another,"
explains McGuire. "There were certain requirements — we needed the Stargate, we
needed a control area, a conference room or briefing room — similar spaces to what
we have in the SGC. And then some multi-purpose areas that could be labs or hallways, that sort of thing. One of the criteria was that it needed to feel very different to
what we had in the SGC." To obtain this different feel, McGuire says she used the
way the set was physically put together to accentuate the two sets' differences. "In the

Above: The city of Atlantis' breathtaking snowflake-inspired design.

SGC, the set is very linear — the control room and the briefing room are stacked on top of each other and they all line up with the gate, and then everything comes off of that at a ninety degree angle. It's very straight, and it's also very dark because we are down twenty-eight levels underground so you get this kind of closed-in claustrophobic feel from the set. So I wanted to go the opposite of that for Atlantis. I set up a dais across the set to maximize the amount of room we had, and then the control room and the briefing room are on an axis off that so that you are looking at the gate at an angle rather than flat on, like in the SGC. Then I just worked out the levels — there's the area underneath the control room and conference room which is a multi-purpose area, a corridor, with the idea that it can be changed around for different rooms depending on what we need."

Of course, the key component of the set is the Stargate itself, for without it there would be no show! For *Stargate: Atlantis*, the producers specified that the gate should be distinctly different, giving McGuire and her team a chance to — quite literally — reinvent the wheel.

"We knew from the beginning that we didn't want the gate that was in the SGC with the ring that spins around, and it's mechanical and runs on a linear bearing. They wanted this gate to be different. It was Paco in the model shop that came up with the idea of using what is basically a ridiculous number of fiber optics and LEDs," laughs the production designer. "They are embedded into a plate, and are all programmed to do a chase, so that the different characters that are made up of all the little fiber optics can appear to move around the gate without any intervention. When he first presented it I thought, 'Oh, that's going to be a nightmare!' It was a lot of work, because each fiber optic thread had to be put into each little specific hole — it was like doing needlework only on a huge scale. But it worked really well. They run it off a PalmPilot which has the different movements programmed into it."

The other significantly different thing about the Stargate in Atlantis is that McGuire has designed it to fold down into the floor of the set. "That's so we can use that space for something else," McGuire explains, "because the gateroom is quite a large part of the 'footprint' of the set. So when we were designing it, we made it so that the gate will fold down into the floor. Also, the back wall is divided into six different panels and they slide back and forth so you can drop the gate into the floor and then change the feature window that is in the back so that it becomes a different space."

An ingenious use of space, maybe, but McGuire admits that with all the work that went into creating the Stargate itself, trusting that the folding mechanism wouldn't damage the most important part of the set caused the whole department a lot of anxiety at first.

Below: A whole new gate to open.

Above: Each part of Atlantis bears the hallmarks of the Ancients.

"The first time that we went to do it, it was a little bit spooky," McGuire admits with a laugh. "We were afraid to do anything, especially since it's our hero element on the stage! If anything went wrong with the Stargate it would be a very, very bad thing! But it goes down very nicely now, you just pop out the panels that are in the floor, drop the gate and slide them back in place."

Though the overall shape of Atlantis itself and the unique style of the new Stargate have served to give the show its own look, much of *Stargate: Atlantis'* substance comes from the minute details added by various members of McGuire's team. The 'bubblers' for instance, tanks of liquid the viewers can see dotted around the city's corridors, taking and extending the theme of water from Atlantis' submerged beginnings.

"The set decoration department made those," McGuire smiles, "and I think they got some tanks off another show. That's something they built in their [model] shop. The glass sculpture inside is something that they took from a bunch of different transparent elements, placed it in there and ran bubbles through them. They look really nice on film. But none of the stuff here is anything you can buy off the shelves in a store. We get pieces and then change them into something that looks fresh."

Another particularly distinctive part of Atlantis' layout is the conference room — far more sophisticated than that in the SGC! The room even has doors that miraculously open together to allow the assembled team members entrance and exit. "All of the doors are on a gear system," the production designer explains, "so it's one guy on the handle manually operating it, and then all the doors swing open at once. They've also got that set up so that we can do that action with all the doors but he can also isolate the doors and have that particular action with just one as well."

As *Stargate: Atlantis'* successful first season progressed, McGuire found herself having to show more and more aspects of Atlantis' sprawling outskirts. Having provided herself with plenty of space to maneuver during the initial design and set up of *Atlantis'* standing sets, McGuire's main concern with shows such as 'Suspicion' and 'Hide and Seek' was to redress the sets in such a way that no viewer would recognize the repeated background. From early on, however, Bridget McGuire and the *Stargate: Atlantis* team had a bit of an ace up their sleeves when it came to set design and decoration, having been bequeathed a massive feature film set. *Blade: Trinity*, starring Wesley Snipes, filmed at Bridge Studios on the 'Effects Stage', which was then taken over to house *Stargate: Atlantis*. Instead of dismantling the massive, solid construct within the studio, the *Blade: Trinity* production simply gave the set to *Stargate: Atlantis*, giving them an automatic head start on some of their sets and helping ensure that the show has some of the highest quality components around.

"We've been using it for our corridors and hallways," McGuire explains. "'Hide and Seek' was one of the first ones where we got to use that. But anytime we're in the Atlantis facility, all the spaces are being dressed and redressed. It looks more extensive than it actually is."

The *Blade: Trinity* set turned up several times during the course of *Stargate: Atlantis'* first season, although McGuire did limit the amount that it was seen on screen for discretionary reasons. "Because we inherited the set from *Blade: Trinity* and that movie hadn't come out yet [when we were shooting] we were trying really not to feature the

Below: Atlantis' conference room.

set itself too much," she says. Nevertheless, viewers can spy glimpses of the set in various forms, most notably in the stunning two-part mid-season story 'The Storm' and 'The Eye', for which McGuire had to build a waterproof set.

"Actually, that went pretty well," McGuire reveals. "We were using what I call the balcony in the *Blade: Trinity* set. The 'bones' of that set are all metal, it's a big metal frame structure. I don't know how on earth we're going to get it out of there when we're done with it, but never

Above: This stunning walk-way was originally con-structed for *Blade: Trinity*.

mind," she pauses, laughing at the thought. "The construction department basically stripped everything down to the frame, put in a waterproof membrane and then built the walls and the floor in front of that. They made sure that we were catching all the water as it was coming down off the rain tower. They set it up so the water would all be funneled down onto the floor and then off the deck into a pool we had below the set, because it was all up on the second level. Then we used waterproof and water-resistant materials to build the rest of the set. When we actually got around to shooting, it was kind of anti-climactic, because everything just worked the way it was supposed to! They were just pounding water down on the actors — they were soaked and the camera crew were all in their waterproof gear. But it went really smoothly. It had to be thought about, but everything was done the way it should be so it was fine."

Fans looking carefully can also catch a glimpse of the movie set when Sheppard runs across a beautifully arched bridge during his attempt to sabotage Kolya's plans. "That's up in the top of the *Blade: Trinity* set, just one of the things that we inherited. I think that's the only time we've seen it — it's in an awkward place to get to. It's up about fifty feet above the ground and you have to go up three levels of stairs, and that's basically the only shot you can get up there," McGuire explains. "So unless it's required in the script for them to be creeping around in something like that, it's not a place that we would go to shoot just for fun! It'll turn up again I'm sure — it's a very dramatic shot." Å

JAMES ROBBINS

R obbins' career started with a Fine Art degree, but he has since turned his exceptional artistic talents to visualizing the beautiful environments, sets and prop components that go into making *Stargate: Atlantis* so stunning. As the show's illustrator, these all start life on Robbins' sketch board, where various ideas take their first physical shape before being passed on to a CG matte painter, set builder or make-up artist for realization. The artist also continues to perform the same task for *Stargate SG-1*, but reveals that working on the spin-off, besides giving him a chance to indulge his love of prosthetic design in his ideas for the Wraith, has opened up a whole new creative world in terms of sets and environments.

Below: Robbins' early poster for the show.

"The whole fantasy/sci-fi thing is a wonderfully imaginative genre of storytelling," says Robbins. "The prospect of being a part of designing new worlds and alien races and their respective technologies was very exciting. The color palettes for the shows are very different, as are our lighting and environments, and it's pretty easy to slide from one side to the other, visually speaking. Continuity is always a concern, especially in episodic television," he adds. "*Stargate SG-1* has spent almost a decade building on the bones of the original movie. We now have a very complex layered database of the history of the shows and the various cultures we have met. *Stargate: Atlantis* is following the same path, building on the new bones of the Pegasus Galaxy."

The first aspect of *Stargate: Atlantis* that Robbins was asked to visualize, and the one that viewers will be most familiar with, was the city of Atlantis itself. "I generated many drawings detailing various aspects of the look of Atlantis, day and night, below water and above. One view was used as a preliminary one-sheet to help in the promotion of the show," says the artist, explaining how his job fits within the larger construct of *Stargate: Atlantis'* behind-the-scenes team. "The executive producers and writers provided their concepts to the produc-

Above: A concept drawing
for the ruined city on
Athosia.

tion designer [Bridget McGuire], who set the overall design parameters. The drawings I produce must work within the established theme. My contributions are in the
execution of those themes. In any concept sketch that I produce for a matte, I try to
emulate the mood, lighting and feel of the scene. Also, as I go through the process of
creating the drawings, concepts occur to me influencing the final product. Bridget and
the producers suggest changes, and more often than not several more drawings will
be produced before we reach the final look. It's a mix of input and contributions from
a number of people that ultimately takes us to the finished product."

Robbins' designs for the Ancient's city grew out of ideas that had been produced
for certain episodes of *Stargate SG-1*, as he explains: "I had a few fleeting images of
underwater ruins, but Bridget had set the look for our Atlantis at the end of season
seven, with 'Lost City'. We were using Frank Lloyd Wright as a jumping off point,
mixed with imagery derived from electron microscope photographs of snowflakes —
the shape of Atlantis viewed from above is from such a photograph."

Of course, the other big component that set *Stargate: Atlantis* apart from its parent
show *Stargate SG-1* was the design of the show's resident 'bad guys', the Wraith.
Designed to be far more physically terrifying than anything the team had come up
with before, it was crucial that their appearance be perfect for the opening pilot
episode. As a result, Robbins says he went though around thirty drawings for the
scarlet-haired Wraith female, and even though nothing like her appeared in the first
season again, the illustrator was more than happy with how she turned out. "She was
integral in establishing the look of the entire race, not merely that single role," says
Robbins. "We continue to tweak and evolve the designs as story elements dictate."

One of those evolving elements was the appearance of the various Wraith ships that the *Stargate: Atlantis* team encountered throughout the first year. Originally designed around the structure of organic shapes such as fragile bird skulls, the artist explains that as the year went on this influence was refined. "Future Wraith ships were also based on the organic shapes found in bird skulls, but the final versions were a little too organic," says Robbins. "Brad [Wright] toned it down a fair amount, making the final renderings of the hive and cruisers more like sixty percent mechanical and forty percent organic. The CGI Wraith fighter, the Dart, is the only ship that is almost exactly as originally drawn. It had a more mechanical feel than the other ships and didn't require the overhaul. It continues to grow," he adds. "As the writers take us into new situations, we become more and more acquainted with our characters. I have recently finished working on designs for yet another class of Wraith spacecraft. Their weaponry has expanded and their history is being developed episode by episode."

Below: A Wraith ship's hangar.

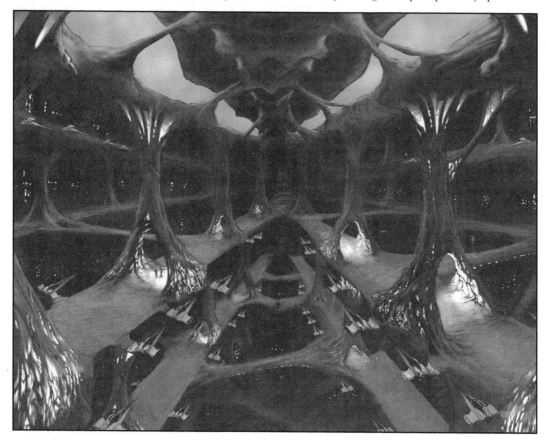

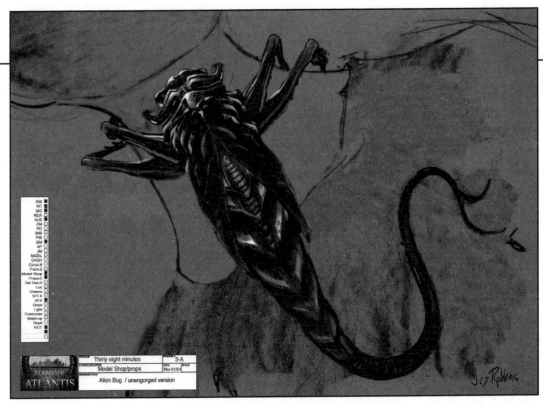

Thirty eight minutes   3-A

Model Shop/props   Mar.01/04

Alien Bug / unengorged version

Jeff Robbins

The artist produces illustrations for both physical (ie sets and props) and computer-generated (ie space craft and alien environments) aspects of the show, and adjusts his techniques according to each medium depending on how his designs will eventually be used. A Wraith stun weapon that will later be made by property master Dean Goodine's model team requires a much more technically specific design than that of a Wraith hive ship to be created by a matte painter in Michelle Comens' visual effects department, for example.

"Virtual environments usually rely on creating the right feel and sense of scale," explains Robbins, "rather than being specifically scaled as required in a measured drawing. A series of measured views must be provided to help accurately create the prop or set, as opposed to a single image for VFX."

Robbins reports that once an image leaves his desk, it rarely changes much on its way to the screen, something that he puts down to the talented team the producers have assembled to work on both *Stargate: Atlantis* and *Stargate SG-1*. "I'm proud of most of the work I do, but not as proud as I am of the people who actually take the drawings I produce and make them real," he says. "The geniuses in the visual effects department, the superb, experienced craftsmen in our paint and construction department, and the unparalleled work of our model shop who continue to make things no one has ever made before. So far I've been unable to stump them, but I'm going to keep trying!" Å

Above: Robbins' illustration for the alien bug in '38 Minutes'.

CHRISTINA MCQUARRIE

Costume designer Christina McQuarrie has worked at Bridge Studios with her team for the past nine years, having first started lending her talents to *Stargate SG-1* before moving on to *Stargate: Atlantis*. Her first task after transferring to the spin-off was to create a new style of uniform for the members of the Atlantis expedition. Whereas *Stargate SG-1* required McQuarrie to be very strict in her sourcing of military styles, with *Stargate: Atlantis*, the rules were a little more relaxed. "Some people might think of it as a military field, but it isn't really," McQuarrie explains. "It wasn't really emulating SG-1 in the sense that the Atlantis team is a civilian [led] group. So we didn't have to look to a military source. It became more like what I call a team uniform."

To create this team uniform, McQuarrie looked at sources far removed from the military lifestyle. "I was looking at sportswear, yoga wear, even motorcycle gear," she says with a laugh. "I was looking at all sorts of different things to generate ideas. You start off with one thing and make a few modifications, but some of the initial ideas were fairly close to where we ended up. The other good thing about the uniform is that because it's civilian based, we are going to continue to modify and change it a little bit because we are not restricted by military codes of dress."

Of course, one member of the team has a distinctly different background to the expedition members from Earth. Teyla Emmagan, though a firm part of Major Sheppard's gate team, isn't shackled by the same dress codes as the rest of the expedition, which gave McQuarrie and her team some scope when coming up with the Athosian's wardrobe.

"Right from the start, we knew that Teyla would become a member of the Atlantis team," McQuarrie explains. "We decided to give her a uniform, but since she returns to her 'home' on occasion, and maintained a connection to her Athosian roots, we also decided that she should continue to wear an element of her original clothing. The blue top that she has worn was actually the under-most layer of her costume from 'Rising'."

In actual fact, this favorite blue top of Teyla's was originally intended to feature far more prominently in *Stargate: Atlantis*' pilot episode, but as McQuarrie explains, circumstances forced a late change of plans: "When I designed Teyla's costume for 'Rising', I did so before I had seen a script, and it was actually a top, pants and vest. As it turned out, much of her action took place outside, and since 'Rising' was shot in February, an over-garment became a necessity! I was very pleased with the coat and we did see a lot of it, but I was sorry that we were never able to remove it and see the outfit underneath. A lot of work went into creating the fabric. The technique we used

Opposite: The cast kitted out in their civilian-based team uniform.

has become a bit of a theme that runs throughout Athosian clothing. However, just by the very nature of episodic television you get used to creating costumes very quickly and never seeing them again!"

The costume department also created a far wider range of costumes for Teyla than the rest of the team, mainly because of the character's display of fighting skills that extended throughout the first season.

"Teyla's role is very physical, but Rachel Luttrell has a strong, toned body, so designing for her is really not that difficult," says the costume designer. "I have tried to emphasize her arms and shoulders and to allow for freedom of movement. Creating her costume for 'Hot Zone' was a lot of fun. We gave her a powerful but very feminine look. Rachel has dance in her background so was not fazed by having fabric swirling around her ankles while performing marshal arts-type movements!"

As the series progressed, McQuarrie's team made other decisions about Teyla's costume that would expand beyond those created for season one. "We also decided that since she makes these forays back to her people she goes on 'shopping sprees',"

Below: Sadly, Teyla's elaborate coat has been seen only once, in 'Rising'.

the costume designer says with a smile. "Later on we see some of the new pieces that she has acquired."

Perhaps the most striking costumes seen during the show's first year, however, were those worn by the Wraith. "I was looking at a lot of artwork," McQuarrie says of her inspiration for the Wraith look. "Actually, one of the first pictures that I put up on my wall was an artistic representation of a bat. Then somehow, I don't know why or how, it evolved from that."

The Wraith seen in *Stargate: Atlantis'* first year came from two distinct echelons of their society, which episode-by-episode determined for McQuarrie whether or not the character would be wearing the distinctive full-length leather coat or not. "The Wraith Warriors are the soldiers of the Wraith world, while the guys in the long coats who we call the 'Male Wraith' are the officers," she explains. "One of the good things is that these coats are made out of very heavy leather, so they will take quite a lot of abuse! People aren't always thinking about costumes when they write the scripts," McQuarrie adds with a laugh, "but surprisingly, this costume, although it does have a flowing skirt, didn't create any problems. It's made in a way that gives freedom

of movement because there's a big split up the back and they've got full pants and boots underneath. So they never actually complained about not being able to do stuff in it — I guess that's a good thing!"

For the Wraith Warriors, McQuarrie turned to her colleagues in the art department to put the finishing touches on their equally menacing costumes: "The warriors were very different. The armor was generated by James Robbins in the art department, who is very good at weird pieces! That whole chest piece has technology embedded in it — although we never really saw it to it's full effect. Then there's the strange mask that's almost calcified bone — a lot of it just comes from the dark corners of one's imagination. Because you just have to keep grabbing things really fast, a lot of it isn't from any real source, you just have a quirky imagination and come up with ideas."

This ability to generate many new ideas helped as the season progressed, particularly when it came to 'The Defiant One', in which Major Sheppard comes face to face with a Wraith who has been trapped in a desert for 10,000 years. "His look is basically a derivation of elements from both the warriors and the Male Wraith," McQuarrie recalls. "But what was very challenging was finding a way of making it look like it had survived for millennia! After much experimentation we developed a method using chemicals that literally ate into the fabric and then we used paint to add depth and texture." Å

STUNTS

JAMES BAMFORD

"I started training in Martial Arts when I was twelve," says Bamford, explaining his own background, "a combination of different styles of Japanese skills, and accompanied by Filipino Martial Arts, Escrima, Kali and kick boxing. I was a competitive fighter in the ring for years." More recently though, these skills have been turned to producing the fantastic stunt and fight sequences seen in *Stargate: Atlantis*.

Whereas *Stargate SG-1* is very much based around explosive action and stunning gun fights, *Stargate: Atlantis* set out to use very different styles of action. "I was told at the beginning that one of the reasons I was brought on to the show was because of my fight background," adds Bamford.

Indeed, one of the stunt coordinator's most distinctive influences on the show has been his work in creating Teyla Emmagan's impressive fighting skills. Originally, Rachel Luttrell's character hadn't been written as the feisty fighter she is now. "When I first got the concept for the show, we didn't know who was going to be cast as Teyla,

Below: Sheppard and Teyla go head-to-head in training.

but it seemed to me from the way the character was described that I could make her into a warrior if I had the opportunity," Bamford explains. "So I talked to Brad Wright about that, and he said, 'Sure, go ahead.' When Rachel was cast, she's amazingly athletic, she's got a dance background and as you can see she's in great shape, so I decided to teach her a couple of different forms of Martial Arts that aren't commonly seen on television or film. She doesn't do any acrobatics — we try to keep her as realistic as possible so that she doesn't do any wasted movement. It's really fast and precise, and she's not high-tech with her weaponry. It stays within her people's realm, as far as she doesn't use anything that can't be found on her home planet. We stick to her short sticks, which we have named Athosian Bantos rods. I taught her knives as well. You also haven't — and probably won't — see her throw any kicks. I'm trying to stay away from things that everyone has seen already. So you'll see knees, elbows, very close fighting."

Bamford credits the success of his plan for Teyla to Rachel Luttrell's ability to learn these new and difficult skills so quickly: "The first day, I just went to her trailer with these sticks and started teaching her some basics — she picked it up in five minutes. And the great thing about her is that she's very keen to learn. She trains on her days off, she always wants to work. Rachel very rarely requires a stunt double, unless it's something extremely dangerous. When you see her fighting on film, it's Rachel Luttrell, not the back of a stunt double's head. Rachel is one of the most natural actors I've worked with as far as physical movement."

Even with Bamford's expertise and Luttrell's natural abilities, filming fight scenes such as the ones seen on *Stargate: Atlantis* is dangerous work. A sequence takes a lot of preparation and rehearsal before it is ready to go in front of the camera.

Above: The rail gun from 'The Siege'.

STUNTS

"I usually choreograph a fight in my sleep," Bamford says with a laugh. "That sounds strange, but I'll get the script and read it just before I go to bed. I'll fall asleep thinking about it, dream about it, and it's odd but I'll usually wake up with half of it choreographed in my head. Then I'll hook up with Rachel and the two of us will get together and slowly I'll go through the motions of what I was thinking about. It seems to progress naturally that way. The two of us will see what works and what doesn't work, because we're not trying to make her a strict Filipino stylist or a strict Japanese stylist — we're letting her create her own style, and she's adding her own. Because of her dance background, she has her own posture, so she adds her own twist to it."

Once the two performers are happy with the sequence and it has been approved

Below: 'The Defiant One' in his 10,000-year old clothes.

by the director and producers, Bamford starts rehearsing. "I like to get four hours of rehearsal for a medium-sized fight, and to shoot it just depends on the schedule. I like as much time as possible, at least twelve hours, but generally you get six to eight hours if you're lucky." Again, Bamford says, the pressures of filming an on-going television show are lessened by Luttrell's own dedication and skill. "Because of her dance background she picks it up really fast and then goes away and practices on her own. I try to keep her training consistent so that when we do something new, she catches on straight away."

Later in season one, Bamford had the opportunity to teach other members of the cast some fight sequences, as Sheppard and Teyla started training in 'Hot Zone' and Lieutenant Ford settled a score in 'The Brotherhood'.

"Rainbow [Sun Francks] is playing a marine, and he's supposed to be a weapons specialist and so on. So I try to keep them completely different style-wise. We did a fight [for 'The Brotherhood'] — we hadn't done one before. He actually did some hand-to-hand, and we used some Indonesian stuff which is more a sort of grappling, joint manipulation style. He did a flying take-down on a guy more than twice his size, and Rainbow has a breakdancing background as well so he took to it amazingly. It's a really brutal, really effective, yet visually appealing cinematic style. So it's something that a Special Forces marine would be taught, but a little more cinematic. We started to teach Joe Flanigan some stick work as well, because Teyla and Sheppard had a little training sequence in 'Hot Zone'. That was a lot of fun, because she was playing his instructor in the scene. He hadn't touched the sticks before because he's all about his P-90, but he picked it up like a natural athlete, like it was nothing."

The 'Hot Zone' sequence itself, Bamford says, is less about fighting skill and more of an exchange between the two characters beyond the meaning of the training itself. "It's really more about the sexual tension between the two of them," explains the stunt coordinator, "the eye contact and the flirting. It's not an intense fight, but it really does what it's supposed to do. It tells the story and it's one of my favorite fights, because the acting is a big part of it and I like to incorporate as much of their characters into the action as possible."

For Bamford, getting as much variety into the action as possible is as important as making sure the sequences are executed accurately, since he believes this makes for far superior television. "Hand to hand combat is more fun because the fights can go on for a lot longer, and what I try to do is have one move flow into the next but without being repetitive," he explains. "So what you'll see throughout the season, whenever you see a fight, you might see a stick and a knife, but the techniques are different. You're not going to see the same fight twice, ever, on this show." Å

Above: Since joining the cast of *Stargate: Atlantis,* Rachel Luttrell has become a proficient fighter.

MUSIC

JOEL GOLDSMITH

I n the world of television and film, music is often left to draw the short straw. Regularly given the smallest budget and the least amount of attention from the producers, film-score music can sometimes be treated as an afterthought. Not so in the *Stargate SG-1* universe, where for several years Joel Goldsmith has produced the beautiful scores that have so enhanced *Stargate SG-1* and now do the same for *Stargate: Atlantis*.

Goldsmith's first task for the fledgling spin-off was to develop a new theme tune. Unlike *Stargate SG-1*, whose tune had been inherited from David Arnold's feature score, *Stargate: Atlantis* would be able to start from scratch.

"I read the script, and it wasn't nearly as Egyptian as the *Stargate* movie," the musician recalls. "Where the David Arnold theme tended to be much more Middle Eastern, with *Stargate: Atlantis* I went for a more pastoral approach, and a little more European. It's still a symphonic orchestra, but it tends to be a more European and Americana approach to the music. Pastoral stuff is not as prevalent in *Stargate SG-1*, although they're not different animals. We wanted to have a tie-in between the two shows because it's still '*Stargate*'. It's the same adventure and the same type of people."

Below: Goldsmith's score helps bring the worlds of *Stargate: Atlantis* to life.

Though Brad Wright and Robert Cooper were happy to let Goldsmith use his talents in isolation to come up with the first version of the *Stargate: Atlantis* theme, both executives did have specific requirements that they wanted to see reflected in the score. "We wanted something thematic and we wanted something that had it's own voice, but we didn't want to re-invent the wheel either," explains Goldsmith. "We wanted to keep the same kind of approach, the adventurous, symphonic approach towards the show. Initially it was left to me to submit my original idea, then once I did that I fine-tuned it for them."

Once the series began production on the rest of the season, the show's score began to expand. Each character began to have his or her own theme which then carries through the year. "Thematically we developed as the season progressed," says the musician. "As things develop new characters often get their own motifs or themes. I would say that Sheppard *is* the *Stargate: Atlantis* theme — that is more Sheppard than anything. Weir has her own theme that plays during the show quite a bit in different places. And then there's a Wraith motif as well."

Developing recurring themes such as these is one way in which a musician can lessen the time it takes to produce a score for a series. With a massive forty-five minutes of script to score for each episode, the time pressures are immense. "I generally have about a week or so," says Goldsmith. "We do have approaches that have been established, and it does make it a little bit easier, but I try to approach each show fresh."

Above: Sheppard and McKay, listening for their characters' themes?

What ideally happens when a score needs to be developed for a script, whether for film or for television, is that the producers will sit down in front of a rough-cut with the musician and watch it, talking through where they think music is necessary, to what degree, and also what sort of style is required. For Goldsmith, who works from his studio in Los Angeles, such 'spotting sessions' have become less necessary over the many years that he has worked with Brad Wright and Robert Cooper.

"The spotting sessions have gotten lighter and not quite as detailed, because we really know what we're doing and we have a relationship now after so many years," says the musician. "But we go over each episode, discuss the show, discuss new characters, and [they are] very specific about their needs. If they want me to bring something out emotionally, if they have something that they want me to cover dramatically, that they feel is perhaps not in the edit, then they tell me." Brad Wright, Goldsmith points out, is also very specific when he thinks a moment would benefit from having no music at all. "You know, silence is very powerful on it's own. He'll often give me a note where he says that he wants the music to come in later, or I'll write something and I brought the music in a little earlier than he wants. Then we generally talk about the amount of music, and where [it should go]. Then I take the show and I just start writing. I generally write from the beginning, right from the top of the show and go

Below: Weir's office, with the Stargate control area in the background.

through to the end. Then we do a Day One mix where we listen and they give changes if there are any. And then I make any fixes that need to be done, and then it's done. If we disagree with each other we simply discuss it, and Brad listens. If he asks for something, and I question it, he re-addresses it and then makes his decision. But he'll always re-address it. But Brad and Robert both know what they want."

Though it would give him more time if he started writing from the day the first draft of an episode is published, Goldsmith reports that it's usually better to wait until the finished cut has been completed. "I write straight from the final," he says. "I see the final cut of the show, and I don't start working until I get that. They send me a producer's cut, but I generally don't read the scripts. Scripts are difficult because you visualize the action in one way and I start writing in my head and all of a sudden I

Above: The female Wraith from 'Rising' gets menacing with some musical assistance.

see the show and it's completely different! So I see the producer's cut, the first cut, and then that gives me an idea of what the show is. Then I don't really start writing until I get the final cut."

Despite the pressured nature of the way he works, Goldsmith says that mental blocks rarely occur, and when they do he has no choice but to work straight through them: "There's really not time for that. If you do get stuck, you just start to rely on something that you've done already. If you're not having amazing inspiration, you learn to write in a different way, you write technically because you understand how to approach something. But generally, the shows are so much fun that you get inspired for them." Å

AFTERWORD

I used to think making one show was hard. A single television series seemed like a full time job at the time... honestly, I thought we were busy. Now that we're making both *Stargate: Atlantis* and *Stargate SG-1* at the same time, with the same writers, producers and department heads, out of the same production office... Well, let's just say that I sometimes think back fondly to the simpler days of producing one series at a time.

As I write this, it's the worst time of the year. We haven't finished an episode yet, but we're thinking about the end of the season already. We haven't yet aired, so we have no idea what the fans are going to say about what we've been working on these past months. At no other time of the year do we have to think about all forty episodes at once. My head hurts.

But this, as they say, is a classy problem. Most television series get cancelled after the first few episodes. Between the two shows, we'll shatter the two hundred episode mark this season, and we're still going strong. There's no question that the two series benefit from each other both on the air and in the sharing of production resources. Although

we occasionally have to stop and think which show we're working on at any given time, or which characters are in any given episode, we've become a fairly well-oiled machine. Our art department has become so adept at sharing stages and sets between series that we've been able to increase our production values significantly. Ideas fly around our story department at warp speed, and even so we barely write them as fast as we can shoot them. The fact is, we're doing things on two shows that would be impossible if we were making just one.

Stargate: Atlantis has been lucky to have an older sibling, just as having a new kid around has breathed life into *SG-1*. Most importantly, fans have responded by watching in ever increasing numbers. It looks like the *Stargate SG-1* franchise isn't going away anytime soon.

Now three shows... That would be crazy. Maybe a movie. Å

BRAD WRIGHT
Vancouver, June 2005

STARGATE
ATLANTIS ™

SEASON 1

A NEW WORLD... A NEW THREAT

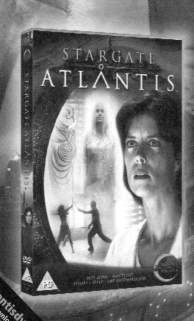

LATEST
EPISODES
ON DVD VIDEO

OUT NOW

ALSO AVAILABLE FROM

TITAN BOOKS

Illustrated Companion series

OUT NOW
Stargate SG-1:
The Illustrated Companion
Seasons 7 and 8

At last,
the original
uncut scripts!
Stargate SG-1:
The Essential
Scripts

WWW.TITANBOOKS.COM